21 Brix

21 Brix

Jim Forchini — Evolution of a Winegrower

James F. Forchini

Michael French Metcalf, editor

White River Press
Amherst, Massachusetts

First published by White River Press LLC,
Amherst, Massachusetts • whiteriverpress.com

ISBN: 979-8-88545-007-2

Book cover and interior designed by Lufkin Graphic Designs
Norwich, Vermont • www.LufkinGraphics.com

Library of Congress Cataloging-in-Publication Data

Names: Forchini, Jim, 1938- author. | Metcalf, Michael French, 1941-
    editor.
Title: 21 brix : Jim Forchini--evolution of a winegrower / Jim Forchini,
    Michael F. Metcalf, ed.
Other titles: Twenty-one brix
Description: Amherst, Massachusetts: White River Press, [2023]
Identifiers: LCCN 2023039959 | ISBN 9798885450072 (trade paperback)
Subjects: LCSH: Forchini, Jim, 1938- | Forchini Vineyards and Winery. |
    Vintners--United States--Biography. | Wineries--California, Northern. |
    Wine and wine making--California, Northern.
Classification: LCC TP547.F67 A3 2023 | DDC 663/.20092
    [B]--dc23/eng/20230925
LC record available at https://lccn.loc.gov/2023039959

Contents

Foreword

OMETIME IN THE AUTUMN OF 2005, my wife, Sharon, and I began to seriously explore the Russian River wine country, and to discover the beauty and tastes of the Dry Creek Valley. One of our more pleasant surprises was the Forchini Winery and Vineyards. We discovered this wonderful small winery during one of the many tasting events which the Russian River winegrowers held regularly to promote local wines to the visiting public. At the Forchini winery, we were met by a fellow directing traffic in the far-too-small driveway access and much-too-limited parking area. He seemed annoyed by the commotion of the day and the crush of visitors, yet he cordially invited us to visit the tasting room. This was Jim Forchini. In the tasting room we encountered a quiet, yet polite, woman who offered us tastes of their wines, which were marvelous. This was Anita Forchini. Thus began our relationship with Jim and Anita Forchini on that happy day, nearly 20 years ago.

As the years passed by, we visited the Forchini winery on many occasions, sometimes for one of their wine events for wine club members, more often just to have a taste of their wines and say hello. Jim was a mechanical engineer; I am a civil engineer. He loved to talk; I like to listen. Anita was an enthusiastic traveler, as is Sharon; they shared their passions for new places to visit and savor. Jim was the winegrower. He directed all vineyard operations and made all the wines. Anita maintained the hospitality side of the business. They fascinated us. They were both pleasant and cheerful, never reserved when it came to making clear their feelings about this or that state regulation, or something the county administration was doing to them and to the local wine industry. In time we got to understand how Jim and Anita ran their business, and we came to appreciate the difficulties they faced and how they overcame adversities. We met their children and granddaughter, who were all very much involved in the family winery. But more importantly, we became friends with two genuinely charming people. Their outspoken nature didn't bother us in the least; we admired their honesty. With our mutual interests and passion for life, we came to appreciate each other. We shared many a cheerful time socially, having a meal in Healdsburg, or at one or other of our homes. We were thankful for the abundance of our lives, and we enjoyed sharing it. It was fun.

In my retirement, I had decided to write about my family and about Sharon's and my adventures over the years. Jim was fascinated by the stories I was telling in print. He was especially impressed that I would write such a family history so that our children would have their family story preserved. He remarked that he should do the same for his family. He thought it would be important to tell the story of how he and Anita became involved in winegrowing, how they persevered and achieved what they had in the last 40 years. I agreed, and I encouraged him to get on with it. "But I can't write," he protested, to which I retorted, "Nonsense. You tell great stories. Just write down what you want to say. I'll coach you along the way, but only if you ask for help." Being one to take on a challenge, Jim seemed prepared to do exactly that. As for asking for help, he never got around to it. Jim had to do it himself.

To my astonishment, about six months later, during the winter months, Jim said he'd drafted several chapters of a memoir he intended to call "21 Brix." Not only that, he proceeded to email me a tranche of 10 "chapters." To Jim, a chapter was a short brain dump, written exactly how this spirited Italian would tell his story. It was quite something to read. It was straight from the heart. And I loved it. So, I urged him to keep going; don't let up. "But every time I set to writing more, I find myself going back and reworking what I've already written. I can't write anything new." I encouraged him to stop fiddling with what he's already done, just keep ploughing ahead. That wasn't something he seemed to want to do: Things had to be polished at every step. With this demonstration of Forchini obstinance, I wondered whether he'd ever complete an initial draft.

Then, in March of 2021, Anita passed away. She did so quickly and was spared much of the pain that she might have otherwise endured. Jim was devastated. He spent many evenings with us at our home in Guerneville, or at his ranch in Dry Creek. After sharing a meal and some wine, he would pour forth his grief. We listened and listened. He no doubt appreciated that we would try and comfort him during his grieving. The matter of 21 Brix came up from time to time. On one occasion he confessed that he had lost his will to push the book further. I told him very directly that was unacceptable, which, of course, he did not appreciate hearing. "Jim, you are writing a memorial to Anita. Don't you dare stop. You owe it to her." His stunned look suggested I had touched a nerve. Perhaps I had gotten through to him.

We didn't hear much from Jim during the holiday season of 2021. He said he had a lot of family obligations to deal with and that we should get together after the New Year. January came and passed into February, and still no word from Jim. A few months later, I sent him an email asking if everything was OK, was it time to get together? Then came the terrible news. Carla, his daughter, informed us that Jim had passed away when crabbing out at Tomales Bay on January 21st. He was chasing after his dog, who had decided to go after something exciting. In pursuit, Jim was stricken with a severe heart attack. He died instantly and peacefully. At least he was out crabbing, something he dearly loved to do.

Several months later I asked Carla whether she was aware of Jim's literary work in progress. She replied that she was, and a month or so later, I received his entire manuscript . . . at least, all he had completed by the time he had passed on. I promised Carla that I would look it over, and I explained that I had offered Jim my assistance should he want it. Now that he was gone, would she like me to pursue further work on the book to see where it might go? Carla encouraged me to pick up the work and do what I thought best.

A quick read of the manuscript indicated that Jim had taken my counsel to heart. His story was essentially complete. Some was in good condition, some not quite so. He simply ran out of time. Most important was that what he had completed sounded just as if Jim was telling me his story firsthand. This was a good story to be shared with a wider audience.

What remained were some missing elements and a lot of cleaning up. I had suggested to Jim that lots of images would help enliven the story. He agreed, saying that he had many good photographs that could be used. A few photographs had been added, but not nearly enough. And the story needed a closing, to explain what happened in the later years of the Forchini Winery days. That closure needed to be written by some members of Jim's family or ghost-written by someone supervised by the family.

With all this work completed, the book would be ready for publication. But the long publication process would require some professional services, which would need funding by someone. I sensed from Carla that Jim's estate would not likely want to fund such work. We agreed that what I could do would be to help complete the missing elements of the story, help collect and insert appropriate images, and copyedit the entire book. In other words, take the book to the point of publishing. My work would be on my account; it would be my contribution to Jim's and Anita's memories. With this understanding, Carla authorized me to proceed with that work.

In his manuscript, Jim makes clear that this is his story, not something to be retold by some writer. The story is written as he wanted to tell it, in his own language and in his own way. He makes it abundantly clear that his story should not be touched. Knowing Jim as I did, I appreciated his sincerity. And I well-understood that damnation would await should I, or anyone else, try and recast his story in some alternative fashion. Out of respect for Jim, that's what I, as editor, have strived to do. Apart from correcting obvious errors (misspellings, confusing wording, peculiar phraseology, and such), what's written is as Jim originally wrote it. It's essentially unchanged. Jim wrote just like he talked: With expression, often with passion. His writing style might seem unconventional to some, but it's authentic Jim Forchini. That is as he would want it, that's how I've edited it. The story as told flows clearly and makes sense. What's important, it's his story. And that's that!

Michael French Metcalf
Guerneville, California
October 2023

CHAPTER 1

Introduction

This Story

THERE HAVE BEEN MANY INFORMATIVE BOOKS written about wine and the wine industry that have covered a wide variety of subject matter. What could possibly be written that has not already been covered a thousand times?

This story is different. It's not about wine types, wine regions, wine tasting, wine and food pairings, renowned winemakers, or historic wineries. In a small part, it's an autobiography. But in a greater sense, it's a story about a husband and wife working together to make a change in lifestyle to become winegrowers, in which neither had any experience. Fulfillment of such a dream would require, on the part of the husband, a transition from a secure and rewarding 15-year engineering career to a new indeterminate career involving risk and uncertainty. On the part of the wife, it would require faith and support in her husband's new ambition.

The term *winegrower* wasn't really used when I made my career change and, in reality, I went from engineering to become a *grape grower*, which by most definitions, was a subtitle of farmer. To most people this might sound like a step backwards, because at the time the prerequisite for a vocation in grape growing certainly did not require a higher education. Some grape growers never finished high school, and a few never finished grammar school because they needed to work to support their family. If you could drive a tractor straight, if you had a strong back and didn't mind physical work, if you could tolerate working under extreme conditions of hot, cold, and rainy weather, if you were willing to risk Mother Nature's impact on your crop, and if you were willing to accept an unknown annual income . . . then you qualified to be a grape grower. Many children of grape growers had no interest to follow in their father's footprints. There were other children, however, who did because of a history of multi-generations of family farming, the love of the land, the agrarian lifestyle, and the satisfaction and freedom of being self-employed.

This story might have an interest for future generations of my family and others who might want to know how and why this bold change came about and what factors led to this dramatic decision. As a husband and father of three young children, the wellbeing of my family was very important. As a wife and mother, the question would be could we provide love, caring, social and health services to our children knowing we would not have company benefits and the security of a sustaining salary? There would be no guarantee of success, only hope and optimism. There would be hard work ahead requiring sacrifices, fortitude, and determination. There would be no business partners, we would have no backup, no bail out. We would be financially on our own to sink or swim.

This story would not have been possible had we not been in the right place at the right time, had I not been of Italian descent, had there not been early experiences in my youth that would later become of influence, had I not been strongly stimulated by a very close friend, and had I not had the complete support and courage from my wife, Anita.

This story is dedicated to Anita, my extraordinary and exceptional wife, who passed away in March 2021 before the publishing of this book. She was my partner in life and best friend for over 60 years of our marriage. Had it not been for her courage, devotion, understanding and complete support, our journey in life would never have taken this course, and this story could never have been written. She was willing to stand by me during my difficult decision to make a change in profession that might threaten the security and comfortable lifestyle of our family of five. We forfeited a good corporate salary with benefits, a comfortable modern home, and bountiful days of leisure recreation, to relocate to an old, neglected farmhouse and face a life of commitment to endless work projects, little play, and financial uncertainty. This we would do in an agricultural industry that had a history of ups and downs, impacted by weather calamities and inconsistent markets. Most wives with three young children would not have put up with it, or have endured it. For better or worse, for richer or poorer . . . , she met the challenge. It took a lot of determination, hard work, and commitment on her part. I was extremely fortunate to have her by my side during this incredible experience of becoming wine grape growers at first, and later co-owners and proprietors of our estate winery.

My hope is that this story will be of inspiration to others. My advice: Don't be afraid to follow a dream, be willing to take uncertain risks, and trust your instincts if you believe in yourself. Time is precious and should not be wasted because it can never be replaced. Don't look back and regret what you should or could have done. If you move forward with caution, do your homework, study the facts, and evaluate all the variables before making major decisions, you will be off to a good start.

This story is authored and written by me rather than an oral history given to a writer. I believe the words had to come directly from me and be written by me in a certain style because it was me who had lived the life, so I alone had to write the words to capture the soul and depth of the experience. I hope you will enjoy reading this story as much as I have enjoyed reliving the memories and writing it.

Some Basics[1]

In a very simple sense, wine will literally make itself. Crush any sweet grapes into a container, mix the skins with the juice and in a few days the native yeasts on the skins will begin to convert the sugar in the juice into alcohol. When the bubbles of fermentation stop . . . you have technically converted the grape juice into wine. The wine may have an overly sweet taste because of incomplete fermentation, might have some pungent aromas, might taste like vinegar, or it might be very astringent . . . but . . . it is wine, like it or not.

This is why the employment of a winemaker who has trained as an enologist is important. He or she will be knowledgeable on all the factors and parameters that can determine the quality of a wine, and can make decisions to avoid defects in the wine that will impair taste and quality. Now comes the secret part. Most employments are defined by a written job description, and the individual's performance is supervised to meet the objective of that description. There are other employments, however, such as an artist, a musician, a singer, a chef, a writer, or an artesian where the individual's creativity and talent are not evaluated by a supervisor but rather judged by public opinion or professional critics. These vocations are expressionistic.

A small estate winemaker qualifies as an expressionistic vocation, because the winemaker, acting alone, will make unsupervised personal decisions to direct the winemaking process towards an identity that connects the wine to the winemaker. Decisions relate to timing of harvest, selection of process equipment, use of cultured yeasts and nutrients, extraction treatment, fining, filtration, barrel selection, aging, and final bottling. This is why the same varietal wines made by different winemakers from the same viticultural area (terroir) will not all taste the same. It's because of his or her winemaking expressionistic style. . . .

Believe it or not!

---

1   Throughout this story, numerous terms of the winegrowing industry are used. To help the reader, a glossary is included at the end of the story. Terms appearing in the text in *italics* are generally explained in the Glossary. Words and phrases in ***bold italics*** indicate where Jim Forchini wished to place added emphasis.

What is Brix?

Brix is a term used to determine the amount of sugar in grape juice. The measurement may be taken using a *hydrometer*, which is a glass weighted bulb with a graduated stem that floats in a container of the juice being measured. The buoyancy of the bulb is directly related to the density of the juice, which determines the Brix measurement as read from the scale on the stem. Another measurement of Brix can be made with a handheld *refractometer*. A drop of grape juice is placed on a glass prism and the angle of light deflected through the prism is read through a lens. The angle of deflection indirectly relates to the brix as read on a graduated scale inside the refractometer. In some cases, the word "balling" is used by older text books in place of the word "brix."

A measurement of *21 Brix* means 21% by weight of the grape juice sample contains sugar; the balance (79%) is basically water and small amounts of organic acids and other organic compounds. *21 Brix* was the sugar base standard for red grapes when I delivered my very first load of Zinfandel wine grapes in September 1971. In general, 55% of the sugar in grape juice can be fermented into alcohol; the other 45% is metabolized into carbon dioxide (CO_2) and heat. In a very basic sense, a ton of grapes (2,000 lbs) at 21 Brix would yield a wine of about 11.5% alcohol by volume, which when fermented dry after pressing would produce approximately 165 gallons of red wine. After racking, filtration, aging, and bottling, a loss of approximately 15 gallons due to evaporation and absorption in the barrels would yield 150 gallons that could produce 750 bottles of wine at 750 ml each from that single ton of grapes.

What Does *Winegrower* Mean?

Winegrower is a term that I have struggled with over the years because of its broad nature, multiple definitions, and the misleading suggestion that you grow wine like some field or fruit crop. Webster defines a *Winegrower* as a person who owns or works in a vineyard or winery, or one who cultivates grapes to be made into wine. The latter definition seems to be the most accurate. A person who cultivates grapes to be made into wine for a long time has been recognized in Sonoma County as a grape grower who owned his vineyard. If you worked in a vineyard but didn't own the vineyard, then you were simply a field worker employed by the grape grower . . . but not a Winegrower. If you worked in a winery as a winemaker, cellar worker, wine salesman, special events coordinator, or in public relations, you were a winery employee, not a Winegrower. Aside from being too broad in meaning, my greatest argument with the use of the title Winegrower is the misleading fact that **you don't grow wine** as implied by the name . . . **you grow grapes,** which not only can be made into wine, but also can be processed and sold as table grapes, raisins, or grape juice concentrate. One of the earliest and most completely ridiculous logos of a Winegrower trade group showed bottles of wine hanging like ornaments from a grapevine, which implied the vine grew these bottles like fruit. It took many years before that logo was dropped in favor of something more appropriate.

Although the term *Winegrower* had long been used in France, nobody really used it in California. The California North Coast Grape Growers Association in 1964, and the statewide California Association of Wine Grape Growers in the 1970s, recognized grape growers and wineries as two separate titles that qualified for voting membership. Schools offering a curriculum in grape growing and winemaking recognized these separate professions by more proper titles: Viticulturist and Enologist. As the industry progressed into smaller defined regions (known as American Viticultural Areas, called *AVA*s), trade associations increased in number and adopted a heavy emphasis on brand promotion and public relations. Professionals in marketing were employed to meet that objective, and the name Winegrowers was adopted from France and was used for promotional purposes of specific AVA regions. These AVA trade associations provided membership for not only grape growers and winery owners, but also offered memberships as associate or affiliate members. Associate and affiliate members could be vineyard management owners, equipment suppliers, transport companies, nurseries, banks, wine consultants, and even hotels and restaurants. I don't believe Webster would be too happy to see hotels, restaurants. or banks referred to as Winegrowers, and I certainly don't think Webster would approve of wine bottles growing from vines used as a symbol of a winegrower. I always favored a better word for a winegrower trade organization—like Wine Producers of specific AVAs. This would distinguish the voting membership of grape growers and wineries from others who were indirectly involved in the winegrowing businesses. These others would be recognized as non-voting associate sponsors of the Wine Producer's AVA. However, I use the term Winegrower reluctantly and honor it because it has been accepted by our industry and has been used extensively.

Identification of Ranches

Throughout this story, several of the wine growing properties owned by the Forchini family are discussed. The three Forchini properties shown on the map of the greater Healdsburg vicinity are called *ranches* instead of *farms,* consistent with convention in Sonoma County. Most agricultural properties in the San Joaquin and Sacramento valleys are called farms. On a Sonoma County ranch, it makes no difference whether you were raising cattle or chickens, or growing prunes, hops, apples, or grapes.

Forchini grape growing properties, greater Healdsburg area.
(Based on GoogleMap GIS, annotated by editor)

Old Redwood Highway Ranch

The 24-acre property, which was acquired in 1971, is referred to as ORH, Russian River Ranch, or Russian River Terrace. The property is located at 12320 Old Redwood Highway south of Healdsburg, California, between U.S. 101 on the east and Old Redwood Highway on the west side. It was the first of our two home ranches.

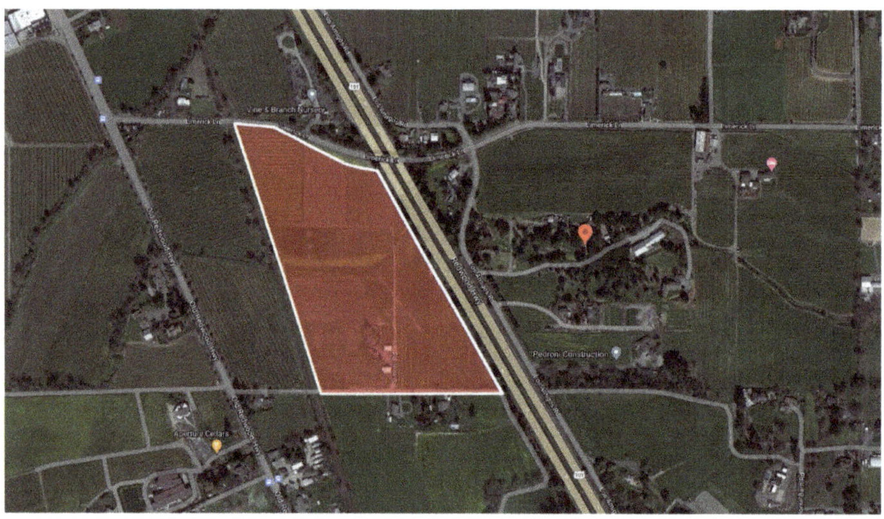

Old Redwood Highway Ranch. Property boundaries approximate.
(Based on GoogleMap GIS, annotated by editor)

West Dry Creek Ranch

The 20-acre property was acquired in 1973. It is located at 9182 West Dry Creek Rd. in the upper reaches of Dry Creek Valley, straddling Pena Creek. No residence was established at this location.

West Dry Creek Ranch. Property boundaries approximate.
(Based on GoogleMap GIS, annotated by editor)

Dry Creek Ranch

The 67-acre property was acquired in 1976. It is also referred to as Dry Creek or Dry Creek Bench. It is located at 5143 Dry Creek Rd in the middle reach of the Dry Creek Valley, on the east side of Dry Creek Road. This was the second home ranch, where a final personal residence and winery were established.

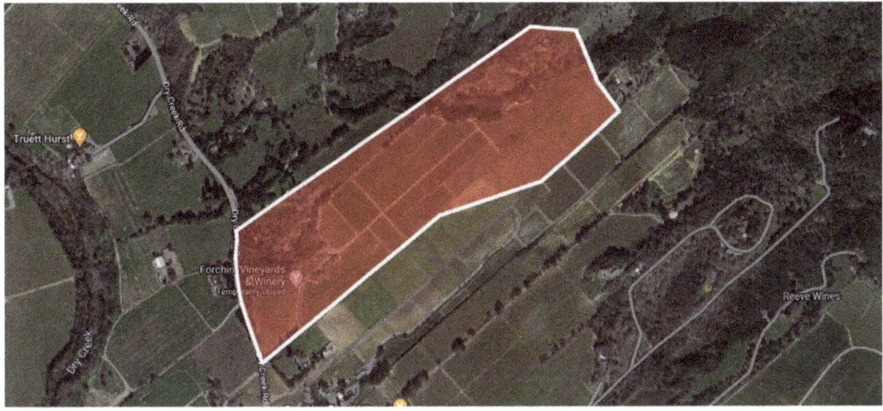

Dry Creek Ranch. Property boundaries approximate.
(Based on GoogleMap GIS, annotated by editor)

CHAPTER 2

Younger Days

I AM OF ITALIAN HERITAGE and was born, second generation, in Bakersfield, California, on October 1, 1938. Bakersfield played an important role in my life, so, after a bit of family history, I'll start there with my boyhood.

Some Family History

Bakersfield was the final destination in America for both my paternal and maternal grandparents. They immigrated between 1906-1913 from depressed northern Italy, seeking lives with greater opportunity. They chose Bakersfield in the southern end of the San Joaquin Valley, where the main economy in the early 1900s was based on agriculture, oil and gas production, and, as the hub of a large rail network, the railroad. These industries offered employment to many newly arrived immigrants. Bakersfield became an important part of my life because grandparents on both sides would raise large families that would remain and work there. Consequently, I had numerous aunts, uncles, and cousins in Bakersfield.

My paternal grandmother, Severina, was from the town of Roasio, located in the northern province of Vercelli in the region of Piedmont west of Milan. In 1906 at the age of 36, she came with four children to join her husband, Giovanni, who had preceded her and was working for the Union Pacific railroad. After arriving, she and Giovanni had two more children before he died in 1911. After his death she operated a boarding house for Italian immigrants who worked mainly for the railroad. It was at the boarding house where she met my paternal grandfather, Giacomo Forchini. He was from the town of Sovere in the province of Bergamo in the Lombardy region northeast of Milan. He immigrated to America in 1908. They married in 1912, and in 1913 Severina gave birth to my father, Frank Forchini. Giacomo worked for the railroad and died in 1936. I never had the opportunity to meet him, but as a young boy I do remember fondly my grandmother Severina, who spoke no English. In 1992 I took my father and my wife, Anita, to the towns of Roasio and Sovere to see the homes where my paternal grandparents were raised. Both villages were notable wine production regions known for dry red wines made from the Nebbiolo grape.

My maternal grandparents were from small villages in the central province of Lucca in the region of Tuscany. My maternal grandfather, Pietro, was born in 1890 in the town of Gragnano about 7 miles northeast of Lucca. He came to America in 1913 at age 23. He was employed by Standard Oil of California as a laborer working in the oil fields. My maternal grandmother, Artemia, was born in 1894 in the village of Veneri near Florence. She was raised in Picciorana, a small village near Gragnano, where she met my grandfather. They had become very close in Italy, and in 1914 my grandfather sent money to Artemia to come to Bakersfield where they immediately married. Artemia gave birth to my mother, Doris (originally named Dora), and then a second daughter and a son. Pietro died in 1976 at the age of 86, Artemia in 1978 at 84. I spent many days with my maternal grandparents during summer vacations as a young boy. In that same trip in 1992, with my father and Anita, I also visited the villages of Gragnano and Picciorana to see where my maternal grandparents were raised, and I explored the surrounding vineyards known for Chianti and Sangiovese wines.

My parents were first generation Italian/Americans born in Bakersfield; my father in 1913, my mother in 1917. They both learned to speak fluent Italian from their parents. After a brief courtship they were married in Bakersfield in 1936. I was born in 1938, my sister in 1942. My father had experience as a mechanic working for his older brother's automotive repair garage in Bakersfield. He later sold automotive products and became a parts manager for a Ford dealership outside of Bakersfield. When the United States entered WWII, he responded to a need in 1942 for workers at the Mare Island Naval Base Shipyard in Vallejo, California. He trained to become a welder repairing Navy vessels. In 1943, my mother brought me and my sister to Vallejo to reunite with him. When the war ended in 1945, my parents chose to remain in the San Francisco Bay area, and they purchased a small house in San Bruno, California, where my brother, Pete, was born in 1946. My father was employed as a parts and service manager with a local Ford dealership, and in time he became the self-employed owner/operator of a Signal Oil & Gas station located on El Camino Blvd. in San Mateo. My mother did the book-keeping for my father's business in addition to being a housewife and raising three children. My parents were both hard-working, middle-class parents, devoted to the wellbeing of the family. My mother died in 1978 at the early age of 62; my father died in 1999 at the age 86.

My Boyhood

My youthful days were normal and consistent with other kids my age. In grammar school, I did well in all subjects, liked sports, and played drums in the school band. Sports included playground baseball, basketball, and some rumble-tumble football in the park, but nothing organized in a league format like today's youth programs. My mother kept me busy around the house with plenty of chores, and weekends normally meant mowing the lawn and doing other yard work. When I was 12, I started going with my father to his service station for a few hours on weekends.

Jim Forchini, age 17,

I entered Capuchino High School in San Bruno in 1952. I took college preparation courses combined with electives in music, sports, and shop. I participated in football, basketball, and track, and became a complete percussionist with the school orchestra. I worked weekends at my father's service station. By my senior year I had a 3.5 overall grade point average, and I started to think about college. Capuchino had wonderful teachers and counselors who made great efforts to seek out students' abilities and interests through a variety of aptitude and vocational tests. This was invaluable, because many of our parents were not college-educated, so it was our school faculty who provided guidance towards higher education and careers. Agriculture was not an option on any vocational tests, since farming had no presence in the Bay Area except a few small dairies and flower farms on the coastline. The results from my aptitude and vocational tests, coupled with my work experience at my father's service station, suggested I might consider a vocation in mechanical engineering. Mechanical engineering seemed attractive to me because I liked automobiles and had had a lot of exposure working on them at my father's service station.

My counselors suggested California State Polytechnic College located in San Luis Obispo, California, which was approximately 200 miles from home. Cal Poly was a highly regarded engineering school and was known for their upside-down curriculum. This meant freshmen took engineering classes in their first year, not during junior year like other schools. A heavy emphasis was placed on "learning by doing," which involved a lot of hours in the shop and laboratory. A Bachelor of Science in Mechanical Engineering required courses in machine and structural design, mechanical drawing, fluid flow, thermodynamics, electrical engineering, machine shop, welding, and surveying, plus classes in higher mathematics, physics, and chemistry. The curriculum was attractive to me. After visiting the campus, which had a lovely setting close to beaches and bays, I submitted my application to Cal Poly in the spring of 1956. I was accepted for admission to the College of Mechanical Engineering starting in the fall quarter of 1956.

Early Influences

There were many early factors that would greatly influence my future as an adult. From adolescence, six seeds that had been implanted within me would later sprout and lead me towards two different vocations.

The *first seed* reflected my two great-grandfathers and two grandfathers, all winegrowers in Italy. Artemia's father was a grape grower in Veneri, and Pietro's father was both a grape grower and bulk wine producer working as a *Contadina* sharecrop farmer with his two oldest sons in Gragnano. Grandfather Giacomo made house wine for my grandmother Severina's boarding house guests, and Pietro made house wine mainly for himself.

The **second seed** recognized wine as a daily staple in Italian culture. Wine was included in all family dinner meals and frequently at lunch. The wine served was nothing fancy. It was usually from a well-known local producer, mostly value-priced, gallon-jug generic dry red wine produced in California's San Joaquin Valley. Sometimes homemade wine was served. On occasion, I remember my aunt having a bottle of Louis Martini wine from Napa on the table, but that was a rare occasion. It was not uncommon for young children to have a little wine heavily diluted with water to celebrate a Holiday meal, and it was on these occasions that I had my first opportunity to taste wine. The women on my maternal side did not drink wine; however, all the women on my paternal side did enjoy drinking wine . . . in moderation.

The **third seed** was sown during the time I spent with my maternal grandparents in Bakersfield. My mother wanted me to have some exposure to old-world values and lifestyle, so she allowed me between the ages of 11–13 to spend extended time alone during summer vacations with my grandparents. While staying with them, I watched my grandfather Pietro leave before daybreak to work in the oil fields, often in oppressive heat, and then return home and spend long hours working until dusk to manage his five-acre property where he grew fruits and vegetables and raised rabbits and chickens. The garden was immaculate with raised beds bordered by earthen curbs, sculptured by shovel and nurtured with compost from his husbandry. His shovels had the appearance of a spade whose point had been worn down to an inverse curve by countless hours of tillage in the garden. I could not help but observe and be impressed with everything he did. He grew table grapes in his garden but would drive to Paso Robles to buy Zinfandel grapes to make his house wine. I observed his winemaking operations in the hand-dug cellar beneath his home. His wines were dark from prolonged skin contact, dry, boldly *tannic*, and high in alcohol. He drank his house wine every day, having one glass for lunch and two glasses with dinner. If the wine became too strong in acidity, he saved it to his vinegar barrel, but for the most part he drank it to the end, or it was used in cooking. But I never saw him pour wine down the drain. My grandfather Pietro was of medium build, mild mannered, soft spoken, thrifty, practical, self-confident, proud, and he was extraordinarily strong. His work ethic had a profound influence on me, and he cultivated an agrarian awareness in me.

Jim Forchini with Pietro (Nonno) Bernacchi (at right) in Bakersfield, ca. 1950.

A ***fourth seed*** was implanted when my mother's sister lost her B29 pilot husband in WWII and remarried. Her second husband was named Tony. He was a B25 pilot, who had returned home after the war to a farm south of Bakersfield. Uncle Tony was from a large Slavic family centered in Arvin, and he grew various produce. I worked for him for during summer vacations in my seventh and eighth grade years. I assembled wire-bound wooden corn crates for shipment to market, and I sewed burlap bags filled with onions. It was this experience where I gained some insight into commercial agriculture, and it exposed me to working with Hispanic farm workers. I developed an understanding of the importance of these farm workers, and I appreciated them as hardworking and fine people, with a strong and binding culture. I was comfortable among them, and this would later serve me well as a winegrower.

The *fifth seed* had been planted by working with my father at his gasoline service station during my high school years. I learned from him how to service automobiles by pumping gas, changing tires, lubricating chassis, and making minor repairs and tune-ups. He had many affluent customers who relied on his services for maintenance of their automobiles. I had the opportunity to drive luxury cars like the Cadillac El Dorado, Lincoln Continental, Buick Roadmaster, and Chrysler Imperial. This experience provided insight into mechanical design and performance. But, more importantly, I learned from my father what it meant to be self-employed, how to run a business, the importance of customer service, and how to build enduring business relationships. His customers varied from upper-class, wealthy, white folks, to working middle-class people, white and minority. My father treated all his customers to the same level of service, and with respect and kindness, regardless of color, race, or creed. All this provided exceptional life lessons for me.

Frank Forchini (at left) and cousin at Signal Service Station, San Bruno, 1960.

The ***sixth seed*** was due to three years of experience working in construction for a major commercial building contractor during the summers of my college years. The contractor was one of my father's gas station customers, who built and remodeled large buildings and structures. I worked as a general laborer, pushed concrete wheel buggies, stripped forms, pulled nails from lumber, and picked up debris for disposal. In my last year I paid union dues as an apprentice carpenter, and I learned a lot about framing construction. Physical labor was never a problem for me, and this experience would be valuable as a homeowner remodeling and building a home, and as a winegrower dependent on extensive physical labor.

College

I arrived at Cal Poly in early September 1956 for campus orientation, freshman welcoming events, and a physical at the campus clinic. I checked-in to my assigned dormitory. I had received a modest $300 scholarship from a local civic group, and with some financial assistance from my parents and personal savings, I could cover expenses the first year. I decided against an enrollment option for Army ROTC since it would delay my graduation by one year and would require two years active duty after graduation.

Cal Poly was predominately an all-male campus until, in 1952, 300 girls joined a male student body of about 3,000. The girls were cloistered in two dormitories on campus, closely watched and supervised by strict dorm mothers, who made sure the girls followed the rules concerning dating and curfew. It also didn't help that the president of Cal Poly lived on campus and had two eligible daughters of age. However, it was clear that the school's top priority was the education of its students.

I lived on campus my first year in a military-style dormitory with two students per room. It was tight quarters. I ate all meals in the school cafeteria. After one year in the unattractive and noisy dorm, I moved out. Actually, I was asked to pack up my drums and leave, after multiple jam sessions with some other musical tenants living in the dorm. I auditioned that year to be the drummer in the Cal Poly Collegians, a dance band following the big band style of Glenn Miller. However, despite my talent, I lost out to the senior class president, who had a beautiful set of Mother of Pearl drums, whereas my set was a mismatch assembly of drums and traps lacking in appearance.

In my sophomore year, I lived with three engineering classmates in a rented older house in town which provided a better environment for living and study, but also provided the luxury to pony up the keg on weekends with classmates. On one dismal weekend I had the flu. My roommates were in Fresno for a Cal Poly/Fresno State football game, so I listened on the radio to the news of Russia's Sputnik satellite circling the globe, which made things better. I attended all major Cal Poly home sporting events and on occasion, took a two-hour drive to visit my grandparents in Bakersfield for a good Italian meal. In my junior year I joined a local fraternity, which provided social and recreational activity, and my drum set found good company with some of my fraternity brothers who were also musicians.

During my junior and senior years, I lived in a large, quiet, and well-maintained home occupied by a widow. I ate dinner meals at a separate private residence and later at the fraternity house. I carried a heavy load; there were many academic quarters of 21 units. In my senior year, I was president of my fraternity and of the Mechanical Engineering Society, whose purpose was to further engineering academics and promote social interaction within the mechanical engineering department between students and professors.

During summer vacations during my college years, I worked part time at my father's gas station on weekends, and full time in building construction during the week. To meet the requirements of my senior project, I recruited two classmates to join me in designing a scale model telescoping chute that would be used by concrete transit trucks to distribute concrete, rather than relying on chutes made up of fixed sections. We fabricated the chute in the Cal Ploy machine shop.

In my senior year in 1959, an event took place that changed my life forever. I was short three elective units needed for graduation, so I enrolled in a course in international economics. While I was sitting in the front row on the first day of class talking with a classmate sitting next to me, a trim brunette beauty, who was obviously a freshman student, came stumbling into class carrying a heavy load of books and binders tightly clutched in her arms. She passed in front of me in a frenzy and I was afraid she might trip. She was late for class, her load had her off balance, and she was in a frantic hurry to find a seat. I was smitten and said to my friend, "Wow! Check out that pie!" In the engineering world. the Greek letter "Pi" is a constant in an equation that relates circumference and diameter of a circle. But in this context, it was a word used by my fraternity brothers to describe any very attractive girl.

There wasn't any time to meet her, because Cal Poly was an expansive hillside campus which meant there was barely enough time to get from one class to the next. A few days later I crossed her path in the campus Post Office and she recognized me from the economics class. I asked if she would like to go to the movies on Saturday night. To my delight, she accepted. No sooner had I made the date than I had to ask her if she would consider a change in plan. I was playing drums in a Western band, and our group had finally gotten an opportunity to play our first gig that Saturday night at a cowboy bar. It paid $10 a man and included beer and food. I asked if she would care to come along, I would spend the $10 to take her out for dinner on Sunday night. She agreed to come and after the music started, to my immediate grief, she became a very welcome guest and was constantly being asked to dance by young barn-stomping cowboys. I worried I might have made a big mistake bringing her to this place, because now I was sure I would have to get in line with these other dudes for dates. But no worry. We went out to dinner the following night, and as luck would have it, we dated steadily throughout my senior year. ***She would be the last date I would ever have!***

Her name was Anita Koerth and she was from Oxnard, California. She was 17 when we first met, and I was 20. She was born in Pearl Harbor on December 22, 1941, 15 days after the attack. Her father was of German descent, born in the United States. At a young age he had returned with his family to Germany, where he grew up. He returned to America at age 17 and joined the U.S. Navy. He was stationed in Pearl as a Chief Petty Officer at the time of Anita's birth. Anita's mother was born and raised in Bremen, Germany. After the war, Anita's family settled in Oxnard, where her father worked in the civil service at the Point Mugu Pacific Missile Range.

Jim Forchini, Class of 1960, age 21.
(Cal Poly Yearbook, 1960)

After taking an average of 18 units a quarter, I graduated in June 1960 with a Bachelor of Science in Mechanical Engineering. Anita was by my side. Cal Poly had an excellent Placement Office, and during my senior year company representatives would visit campus to interview young engineers. I was offered a job with Westinghouse Electric in Pennsylvania working on turbine development. The offer was good for 30 days, but I held off, looking for something closer to home. I was next offered a job with a large construction company in Los Angeles, but the job didn't appeal to me because I had been involved in commercial construction and wanted something different.

Graduation date was fast approaching. I hadn't found a job, and I was getting anxious. In late May, a fantastic job opportunity came up with the Jet Propulsion Laboratory (JPL) in Pasadena, California. The chance to work in aerospace would be cutting-edge, and I quickly accepted. Without any break after graduation, I began work at JPL in July 1960. I was eager to start working and earn some money after four years of college on a spartan budget.

JPL

President John F. Kennedy had made the commitment to put a man on the moon in 10 years. JPL, under supervision of the California Institute of Technology in Pasadena, held the NASA contract for unmanned space exploration. Their contract covered studying the lunar surface and its environment and sending out research satellites to other planets. I was 21 and single, and I was facing the military draft. JPL wrote a letter to my draft board stating my importance to the space exploration program. I was granted a deferment.

JPL designed the Ranger spacecraft and the Surveyor lunar land explorer. Subassemblies, components, and operation controls were subcontracted to companies all over the United States. I worked in Contracts and Procurement writing contracts, work statements, and purchasing component hardware for final assembly on site at the JPL Space Craft Assembly Building. I was surrounded by top scientists and would see numerous important people when they came to the Laboratory. I had my own office and personal secretary. I would be shuttled to Los Angeles International Airport by JPL helicopter for travel back East to review sub-contracts on liquid bladder expulsion projects with Minnesota Mining, and for rocket testing at Thiokol Chemical in New Jersey. There were JPL helicopter flights to the Mojave Desert to inspect our Deep Space antenna installations at Goldstone, and mid-course rocket propulsion testing at Edwards Air Force Base. I flew by JPL Aero Commander to Ryan Aircraft in San Diego to inspect development contracts on the spacecraft solar panels. My activities and opportunities the first year out of college were enormous. They provided for me experiences most engineers starting out fresh would not receive until later in their careers. Work at JPL was exciting.

Life was good, my family was proud of me, and I was respected by those who knew I worked at JPL. My salary easily covered rent, food, and personal expenses. I had excellent health, vacation, and sick leave benefits, and I had no student loan debt. I shared an apartment in Arcadia, California, with an aeronautical engineer named Dean, who was a former classmate and fraternity brother at Cal Poly. Our apartment was within walking distance to the Santa Anita racetrack, and on occasion I could walk in free to catch the last two races. Dean worked at Convair Aircraft, and spoiled himself by buying a Fiat Alfetta sports car so he could show off his status as a rocket engineer. Not to be undone, I parted with my 1953 Ford and purchased a Sunbeam Alpine roadster made by the Roots group in England. I placed a NASA logo decal on the windshield so that I could show off my connection with outer space exploration. My Alpine got me up to Cal Poly fast on the weekends to see Anita, who had entered her sophomore year, or to Oxnard when she was home for holiday. I was living large. My decision to go to Cal Poly to earn an engineering degree and get an excellent job with good salary was paying off. It was a dream come true.

Anita Forchini at wedding, San Luis Obispo, 1961.

In December 1960 I proposed to Anita. After 15 months of courtship, she knew my family, and she knew everything good and bad about me. She unconditionally accepted my proposal. She completed her winter quarter at Cal Poly, and we were married in April 1961 in the historic Mission San Luis Obispo surrounded by classmates, friends, and family from both college and home. We settled in a small apartment in Pasadena, and she found a job as a secretary with an aerospace company that manufactured aeronautical wiring harnesses. She also continued her education at Pasadena City College for credit courses towards a BA degree in English. I continued my education, taking night courses at UCLA in a business management program for technical personnel, and a course in Government Contract and Procurement procedures.

It was difficult for Anita to drive the Alpine for shopping and errands. She had a driver's license, but never had her own car to drive and had very little driving experience. We practiced her driving in the parking lot of the Rose Bowl, but I soon concluded the manual 5-speed transmission of my Alpine could not endure much more clutch and gear abuse. It was not a practical car for us at the time, and with regrets, I sadly sold my Alpine. I gave up high performance and Euro-styling, and downsized to a new 1962 Ford Falcon with automatic transmission. But this car was easier for Anita to use. We drove our new Falcon to Seattle and back to see the 1962 World's Fair and visit Cal Poly classmates who were working at Boeing Aircraft in Seattle.

Unknown to us, after crossing the Golden Gate Bridge and heading north on U.S. 101, we would go through Healdsburg, California, and would pass within close proximity to a farm property which we would eventually purchase nine years later in our beginning experience as Winegrowers.

Although I loved the people and my job at JPL, the prospect of living and starting a family in Southern California did not appeal to me. It had beautiful surrounding mountains and wonderful beaches, but the Loa Angeles basin was handicapped with poor inland air quality, ribbons of congested freeways, highly crowded contiguous cities, and a monotonous dry climate of fair weather without seasonal change. I was longing for northern California and the Bay Area where I was raised, and where I could go and root for the San Francisco Giants and 49ers rather than the Los Angeles Dodgers and Rams.

In 1963, a good friend named John Matteucci paid us a visit in Pasadena while he was on his honeymoon. John and I were both mechanical engineering students at Cal Poly and had worked together on our senior project. After graduation he took a job with a company in Santa Rosa, California, that applied vacuum-deposited thin films on components for both defense and commercial application. He liked the company and had quickly become a department manager. I asked him about employment opportunities with his company and if they were hiring. He put in a good word for me, and I received a call to come up for an interview. I was offered a job, but the salary was 5% less than I was currently making at JPL. I accepted the job thinking it would be worth being back in northern California, and I believed I could make up the difference in salary in a short while. So, after three years with JPL, I sadly gave notice and left in May 1963. Then we quickly relocated to Santa Rosa where I began work with Optical Coating Laboratory (OCLI). I would miss the excitement of being directly involved with NASA and outer space exploration. But my heart was in the Bay Area, and we were now heading for Northern California.

As it turned out, OCLI would become my steppingstone into the wine country. I would be working and living within the famed North Coast wine region of California, which included Napa, Sonoma, and Mendocino counties.

OCLI

I began work at OCLI in June 1963. OCLI produced a wide variety of coatings for controlling both light and radiation. Coatings were made from elemental oxides, metallic compounds, and noble metals evaporated under high vacuum in stainless steel coating chambers. The coatings were deposited on glass substrates by an evaporation process in ceramic crucibles using radiant filament heaters, conductance heating through high temperature metal boats, or by electron bombardment. OCLI's most important proprietary coating was an anti-reflection coating that could reduce the reflection of a glass substrate. When applied to both surfaces, the transmission of light was nearly 100%; the substrate became almost invisible. Other coatings produced by OCLI were multilayer coatings to control lasers and specific wavelengths, cold mirror coatings used by the dental industry, electric conductive coatings for defrosting aircraft windows, and other coatings to transmit or reflect infrared or ultraviolet light.

I spent a few months operating various coating machines to gain an understanding of the overall process. Then my job was to design tooling for substrate supports that would enable uniformity of the applied coating over the substrate. I also worked in research, reporting to two physicists, developing coatings and working on vapor deposition methods. My most important assignment was setting up a high-efficiency anti-reflection coating system on location with a large glass company in Michigan. I instructed their personnel on how to operate the vacuum coating chamber and produce the coating.

Anita and I lived in an apartment at first. I carpooled to work with other nearby OCLI employees while Anita resumed her education at Sonoma State University. In 1964 we purchased a vintage two-bedroom single-bath home with a small lot in an established older neighborhood near Santa Rosa Junior College. The home had been used as a rental and needed many improvements and repairs. I spent weekends and nights remodeling the kitchen and bath, paneling, painting, and attending to outside yard landscape projects. My prior construction experience served me well.

Five years into our marriage we became proud parents when our first son, Michael, was born in January 1965. Anita's aunt and uncle were temporarily living with us, having just relocated from New York. This allowed Anita to go back to school and finish her bachelor's degree in English, which she received in June. In 1966 we sold our remodeled house at a good profit and purchased a newer three-bedroom, two bath home on a lovely half-acre country lot adjacent to a seasonal creek in Santa Rosa's Rincon Valley.

After four years I was becoming disappointed with OCLI, and my interest in coating products was diminishing. The coatings OCLI produced were not something that could be seen, handled, or touched; they were of zero mass and had no moving parts. Other than the equipment and tooling used to make a coating, the final product was not mechanical in nature. I simply wasn't interested in being a plant engineer in charge of machinery or tooling. Furthermore, my friend John was doing well as manager of the anti-reflection production department, where he was entitled to daily lunches in the Company staff room and was granted stock benefits. I had only received cost-of-living salary increases over four years, yet I had not recovered the 5% drop in salary I had received at JPL. The workplace environment was not very desirable. My office consisted of a desk set against a blank wall in the main production building, which was windowless and filled with production machinery that created a consistent level of high background noise from vacuum pumps, motors, and pneumatic actuation cylinders. I had not progressed to any managerial position after seven years out of college. I wasn't where I thought I should be. So, I began to think about a change in employment. Yet I knew a change would probably require a relocation from beautiful Santa Rosa to a larger Bay Area city where technical employment opportunities were more available.

I began looking for engineering employment opportunities in the classified sections of the *San Francisco Chronicle* and the local newspaper. To my amazement I discovered an ad seeking a New Product Development Engineer with Fluor Cooling Products located in Windsor, which was only 10 miles north of where I was currently working. I quickly arranged an interview to meet with the vice president of engineering late one afternoon after work. His name was Don. He had graduated from the University of California, and I found him to be a dynamic mechanical engineer, with vision and bold ideas. He told me he had recently hired a manager for Fluor's newly created New Product Development (NPD) department, who would be arriving from Illinois very soon. I would be part of the new NPD. I was excited at the prospect, and I thought might have found exactly what I was looking for. I was impressed with the goals and objectives of the NPD Department and was glad I would have the opportunity to get in on the ground floor developing designs for proprietary mechanical machinery and components.

I was offered a job and immediately accepted the position of New Product Development Project Engineer reporting to the Manager of the NPD Department, at a 5% increase in salary. This made up for the loss in salary from four years ago. My job description would include project assignments working on design, development, and manufacturing of mechanical products that were currently being procured from outside sources. I resigned from OCLI on June 16, 1967, and lost no time starting employment with Fluor Cooling Products on June 26, 1967. I was happy that that no relocation would be necessary because we were comfortable living in our new Santa Rosa country home, and we would have regretted having to leave this lovely area of Sonoma County.

Fluor was my third employer in seven years out of college. What's more important is that I would now be working well within the North Coast wine region of California, where Anita and I were happy to be living.

Fluor/Ecodyne

Fluor Cooling Towers was a division of Fluor Corporation, a major international engineering contractor headquartered in Los Angeles. They designed and built industrial process plants and electrical power plants, which used cooling towers to reduce circulating water temperatures in the control of mechanical equipment. The towers were used by the petroleum industry, and by electrical utilities in their nuclear, coal, and gas-fired power generation plants.

The manager whom Don had hired to supervise the newly created New Product Development Department was named Sam. Sam arrived two weeks after I started, and I was looking forward to meeting him. He was from Chicago, eight years older than me, and had previous experience in both design and manufacturing. My impression of him was favorable. He was down-to-earth, pleasant in personality, and unpretentious. I could see that I would enjoy working with him.

Don's Engineering Department also included departments for Thermal and Structural. Thermal would evaluate design options that potentially could meet the customer's cooling requirements. Fluor's new cooling tower products were intended to be incorporated into larger process plant designs in which Fluor was involved. Structural would design the basic shell structure of the cooling tower, which would be constructed in either wood or concrete. The tower structure would include mechanical components such as fans, fan exhaust stacks, gearboxes, electric motors, motor and gear supports, fill packing, fill hangers, joint connectors, large diameter piping, pipe valves, and nozzles. All of these mechanical components were part of systems for distributing large volumes of high-temperature process water and reducing the water temperature by evaporative cooling. Process water would be pumped into the top of the cooling tower and distributed to open basins above the fill packing. The fill packing broke the process water into spray patterns as the spray flowed downwards through the fill packing. The process water was broken into droplets that enabled efficient heat transfer to air drawn in by the fans. The cooled process water would exit the tower at a lower temperature, and the warmed air would be discharged to the atmosphere. Don had some creative design concepts for these new cooling tower products, which could be manufactured in-house or procured from others.

It was Sam's and my responsibility to help meet Don's product objectives. Neither Sam nor I had any prior experience in the design of fans or gearboxes, but design literature on various types of gears was readily available. We were both mechanical engineers and knowledgeable in stress analysis, machine design, and strength of materials. While we had little experience, we knew how to do the research and find the information we needed. On one occasion, I visited UC Berkeley to confer with an aeronautical engineering professor who introduced me to airfoil concepts of airplane wings that I could apply to fan blade design. I had responsibility for the mechanical design of a family of single-reduction herringbone gearboxes, some quite large (up to 300 hp, 30' diameter, capable of delivering 100,000 cfm). The fan designs included determining the shape of the fan blade cross-section, developing the taper and twist of the blade from hub to tip, and the structural design of an internal structural spar. I also had design responsibility for the fan hubs, motor and gear supports, and I oversaw the preparation of mechanical drawings prepared by draftsmen. Sam worked on molds and tooling to fabricate the fan blades, which were foam-filled fiberglass castings. He also designed fan stacks, control valves, nozzles, fill design, and hangers. Don, Sam, and I got along very well together, and we would regularly get together to go over design and development of these new products, and to review each other's work. It was exciting and challenging to collaborate on design, exchange ideas, and discuss manufacturing options. I had an enclosed office with a large window that looked outside. Don, Sam, and I all shared the same secretary.

Our daughter, Carla, was born in December 1967, and we were now a growing family of four. My salary had increased every six months, and both Don and Sam gave me good reviews on my performance. I was happy with the decision I had made to leave OCLI. Anita and I joined a swim and tennis club which was a short walk from our country home, and we invested in a 25-year Forest Service lease that included a rustic cabin at 5,600' elevation on Pinecrest Lake on Sonora Pass Highway 108 in the Sierras. We used my company vacations and many 3-day holidays to go to Pinecrest, where we could swim, backpack, fish, and sail my El Toro sailboat.

Within two years after my start with Fluor, the company was sold to Trans Union Corporation, a Division of Union Tank Car Company headquartered in Chicago. The Fluor Cooling Products name was changed to Ecodyne Cooling Products. All former Fluor personnel remained in place with the exception the former Fluor President, who was transferred to Fluor Corporation in Los Angeles. He was replaced from within by the former Vice President of Marketing, who would now become President of Ecodyne. I liked working at Ecodyne and interacting with the other departments for marketing, procurement, construction, and administration. There were good people working there in all departments, and there were many opportunities involving company entertainment, social get-togethers, business lunches, dinners, golf games, and travel.

Life was good and I was thankful for all the good fortune that had come my way.

A Friend Named Bruce

At 9:45 am each morning, a canteen truck would appear in the company courtyard and beep its horn to announce its arrival. People from various departments would flock to grab a cup of coffee and pastry, talk business, and interact socially. It was there that I first met Bruce, who was Ecodyne's contract administrator. He was very friendly and interested in the new products coming from the New Product Development department. He administered the contracts that included our new product designs, which were being erected all over the country. He was always happy and pleasant, never expressing any discontent, and I always enjoyed talking with him. We became close friends both during and after work.

Bruce was five years older than me, born and raised in Santa Rosa, in a large, extended family whose business was farming and related agriculture support services. He had married his high school sweetheart and had three children. He had worked for Fluor almost all his professional life since graduating from high school. His father had a 10-acre prune orchard and a French Colombard vineyard located northwest of Santa Rosa off River

Road. Bruce leased his father's property, and I learned from Bruce that, with a little effort, one could earn some extra money by growing wine grapes on the side. In those days grape growing practices were simple and not as demanding in detail as would be the case some 40 years later. If it was as simple as Bruce said, I thought I might be interested in some extra income for my growing family. Growing things wasn't foreign to me, and I was not afraid of putting forth a little extra effort. Anita and I grew vegetables and flowers on our half-acre country home, I had exposure to agriculture from my grandfather and from working on my uncle's farm as a young boy. I also drank wine and thought it might be worth looking into growing wine grapes, which would give me the opportunity to make a little wine for personal use while earning some extra money on the side.

Bruce made it sound simple. He explained that you had four months over the winter to prune the vineyard, which could be easily done yourself by working on weekends, holiday breaks, and in after-work hours. When spring arrived and the ground was ready, you would apply fertilizer and then cultivate the vineyard two to three times to remove the winter cover crop. Three times over a period of 4–8 weeks, his 10 acres needed to be disced in one direction and then cross cultivated. The two-part operation would take about three hours, requiring about 18 hours of tractor work. This was followed by removal of unwanted shoots at ground level (called "suckering"), and by hoeing around the vines. A lot of this work could be hired out using part-time migrant workers.[2] Bruce went on to explain that between June and August, you gave the vines a dusting of sulfur every 2–3 weeks to control mildew; his 10 acres could easily be dusted in an hour by using a tractor-mounted duster. After that, it was simply a matter of waiting for the grapes to ripen, which would usually occur around mid-September. You would then recruit a migrant harvest crew and harvest the vineyard during your company vacation time. With favorable weather, you could finish harvest in a week, then take a break until starting over again for the following year. If you were anxious to get going, you could start pruning in November, otherwise, you would wait until after the holidays to begin operations. Your grape payment would normally come before the end of the new year.

It sounded too simple. But Bruce was happy, and his family was doing well. The other positive aspect would be, in addition to a little extra income, grape growing would give me the chance to stay physically fit, and it would provide a healthy outdoor environment for not only me but also for my family. I realized it might compromise our free time spent at Pinecrest, but maybe we could strike a good balance between the two. I was starting to think about the prospect of growing grapes.

---

2   Migrant workers were easy to find. Many of them were here as a result of the Bracero program in California between 1958–1964. Others were new migrants who would assemble at various locations around Santa Rosa looking for work.

On an extended lunch break in the summer of 1969, Bruce and I looked at some winemaking equipment for sale that Anita had noticed in the classified section of the local paper. With this basic equipment, we thought it might be fun to try our hand at making a small batch of wine from grapes that we would be able to get gratis from Bruce's father's vineyard. Gordon, who was a mechanical engineer and close friend working in the Thermal Department, thought he might like to join us in this venture, so the three of us got together and bought the equipment, which included a large open-top, half-ton-capacity redwood vat. This vat would be our *fermenter*. We used Petite Sirah grapes and crushed them by hand using a roller crusher. The macerated grapes containing stems and seeds were placed in the fermenter. The grape skins contained the native yeasts that were critical to *fermentation*. The fermenter was covered with a tarp and placed outdoors near the vineyard. Once a day we *punched* the cap down into the juice to extract color and flavor. It took forever to ferment because of the wide variation in outdoor temperatures. We used no nutrients and the *native yeasts* struggled very slowly to convert the sugar into alcohol. After about four weeks, fermentation activity appeared to stop, telling us we now had wine. We drained the juice and pressed the skins by hand as we transferred the wine to a 60-gallon barrel. The wine turned out to be very dark and *tannic*. However, we were hoping it would smooth out in time with barrel aging.

The barrel was placed in Bruce's garage, where periodically we would taste barrel samples to monitor the wine's development. After six months we started to notice the structure of the wine was becoming weaker in body, lighter in color, and was tasting diluted. Suspecting something wasn't right we pondered what could cause this change. In short order, Bruce's fatherly instincts led him to suspect his teenage son might have been thieving from the barrel. Soon, we were able to obtain a confession from his son that he had been siphoning off a little wine for himself and his buddies, and would top off the barrel with water to cover up the lost content. Rather than being upset, we were pleased that at least someone thought the wine drinkable. We bottled a few gallon jugs, discarded the rest, and this became my first attempt at making wine from crush to bottle.

After this experience, neither Bruce nor Gordon wanted anything more to do with wine making. I purchased their share of the equipment, thinking maybe I might use this equipment someday to make a better wine. I started to think about buying some property with a small existing vineyard. This would not only be a real estate investment but also would provide the opportunity to earn some extra money growing grapes on the side, just like Bruce was doing. I wondered how this venture might sound to Anita and if she would be in favor.

CHAPTER 3

Part-Time Winegrower

I REALIZED THAT ANY INVOLVEMENT I might consider as a part time grape grower would have to be small, because my first allegiance was to my job and Ecodyne. Ecodyne was my primary source of income and provided health and vacation benefits for the family. I would seek out a small vineyard, but I had no idea what was available or what agricultural property cost, because I had never looked. Bruce leased his father's vineyard, which gave him an advantage because he didn't have to make loan payments on a vineyard or pay property taxes. Regardless of Bruce's unique situation, I could not stop thinking about maybe doing a little grape growing.

A Man Named Simoni

On a sunny midweek October day in 1970, rather than using my lunch break to play cards with the usual group in the drafting room, I took my brown-bag lunch, jumped into my car, and drove north up Old Redwood Highway, the former U.S. 101 before the freeway was constructed. I paid a visit to the father of my friend at Cal Poly, John Matteucci. John's father owned and operated a small grocery market south of Healdsburg. I had previously met him at Cal Poly in June 1960 when John and I graduated. Not knowing if he would remember me, I introduced myself as Johnny's friend from Cal Poly. After a moment he smiled and said he remembered me and wanted to know how I was doing. I reminded him that I had worked with John for four years at OCLI, but I had left the company three years ago and was now working at Ecodyne about seven miles south of his market store. I said I liked my new employment, my family was well, and that I saw John on occasion. I explained that because of an acquaintance at work, I was becoming interested in grape growing as a side venture to my principal occupation. Mr. Matteucci had been a long-time resident of the area, and because his store serviced nearby residents, he knew practically everyone.

He also had a small vineyard and prune orchard behind his store and knew a little about the economics of raising grapes and prunes as a side venture. He gave me a slight smile—clearly meant not to discourage me—and said he heard there might be a nearby property for sale just up the road. But he wasn't certain. He advised there was no signage indicating property for sale, but he gave me some general directions. He advised I go north about a mile and look east for a tall white enclosed water storage tower, which would mark the general location. I thanked him for his time and headed up Old Redwood Highway looking for a white water tower.

For sure, I was entering wine country as there were vineyards on both sides of the highway. I drove slowly north observing the vineyards, which actually distracted me from my priority of looking for the water tower. When I got to the Foppiano Winery, I hadn't seen any water tower and thought maybe I had gone too far, or had missed it, so I turned around and slowly retraced my route south, when off to the East I spotted a white water tower in the distance. At a small green house on the left of the highway was a narrow, unsigned, and unpaved road that led in an easternly direction towards this water tower. I turned left onto the road and drove slowly. On my right was a small vineyard that appeared to be part of the property belonging to the green house, and on my left was a larger vineyard without any noticeable buildings. I continued slowly until I crossed the Northwest Pacific Railroad tracks, which had a stop sign but no crossing or gate control. After crossing the railroad tracks, I passed between a row of beautiful old prune trees lining each side of the road. Extending beyond both rows of trees were some magnificent old-vine vineyards. The water tower was now in clear view. But I did not see any "For Sale" sign. I kept going and soon reached a small white house on the right. Across the road from the white house was a gravel road that led directly towards the water tower.

Turning left onto this road, I entered a spacious, unpaved yard area. It was clear that the water tower was a part of a large farmhouse located on the northwest corner of the yard. Planted close to the farmhouse were fruit trees and a small vegetable garden. In addition to the farmhouse, there were other buildings, hutches, and pens bordering the yard. On the south side of the yard was a 24' × 40' wood-framed, 3-stall barn with a steep pitched corrugated steel roof and track-mounted roller doors. Multiple pigeon boxes were mounted on the front of the barn. A detached 12' × 36' building on the north side of the yard had a steel roof similar to the barn and was enclosed on two and a half sides with stucco. The building served as an open-sided garage for a Model B Ford coupe, a late model Chevy compact sedan, and a 1949 flatbed 1½-ton GMC truck. On the far east open corner of this building was a strange-looking brick furnace structure with an articulating overhead steel frame that maintained a large 3' × 4' steel basket. I could only wonder what this apparatus might be used for.[3] Around the perimeter of the open yard was a weathered small redwood-sided shed that housed a tractor and vineyard tools, a graduated glass-bowl gasoline lever pump, a fenced chicken pen, a rabbit hutch, a 5-ton steel grape gondola mounted on a wooden stand, and various detached agricultural implements. Strewn about was abandoned farm equipment, all left uncovered. Surrounding this open yard and buildings were blocks of old vineyards and prune orchards separated by dirt avenues.

Louie Simoni, ca. 1971.

Standing In the middle of the yard as I drove in was stocky older man carrying a water pitcher. He looked to be 70 years in age or more. He had the weathered look of a farmer; his complexion was wrinkled and ruddy, and his unshaven face carried a four-day stubble. His name was Louie Simoni. He was in the process of feeding his rabbits. He was wearing a long-sleeve brown khaki shirt and pants, and a tattered old sweater. His head was protected with a field cap. By contrast, I was wearing slacks with a dress shirt and tie. As I stepped out of the car to approach him, he gave me a stern and intimidating look, clearly wondering who was this stranger who just drove up? . . . And more importantly, what did he want? I realized that I was an unsolicited visitor, maybe even considered a trespasser. So, in a polite, but nervous manner, I explained that I had stopped at the nearby market, and Mr. Matteucci had referred

me in a general direction to this property, on the belief the property might be for sale. I explained that I had not seen any sign, so I cautiously asked him if the property was for sale. He paused for a minute, pondered my question, then answered in a reluctant and gruff manner, "Yeah, the property is for sale." But he wanted to know who I was, and where I was from. I explained that I lived in Santa Rosa, that I was an engineer working close by in Windsor, that I was second-generation Italian, and that I was considering buying a small vineyard to become a part-time grape grower. He gave me a wry smile and a brief chuckle. But once he realized I wasn't the scion of a local family, he softened his tone and answered some basic questions. I was interested in knowing the acreage, price, plantings, if any farm

---

3   I later learned the function of the brick furnace and articulating steel apparatus was a prune dipping facility. It included a 3' × 4' rectangular steel basket which could be lowered by hand lever into a steel vat of lye and boiling water which would soften prune skins before they were set out to dry in the open sun on large redwood trays. The vat was heated by wood fire within the brick furnace.

equipment was included, where he sold his grapes, and whether I should be speaking with a real estate agent who might be handling this sale. He gave me brief answers to my questions: He sold his grapes to Allied Grape Growers, a cooperative operating in Asti at the former Italian Swiss Colony plant; and he was selling the property "By Owner".

I was overextending my lunch break and needed to go, so I thanked him for his time and asked if I might return and speak with him to learn more about the property. He agreed. But I really believed he thought I would never come back.

Let's Do It

After meeting with Simoni, I was anxious to tell Bruce what I had discovered and was eager to show him the property to get his opinion. He too was interested in seeing the property since he was mostly familiar with vineyards in the Fulton area of Santa Rosa where his father's vineyard was located, and he did not have any exposure to vineyards in the Healdsburg area.

But when I told Anita what I had found, she cast a frown and displayed a less-than-encouraging attitude about the whole idea of buying a vineyard. In the back of her mind, I could tell she was concerned about the impact this might have on our family and lifestyle. Our life was nicely balanced between my work at Ecodyne, with weekends, holidays and vacations free to go to Pinecrest, the swim club, and other family outings. The question of buying a vineyard might interfere with those family pleasures, or it might eliminate those pleasures all together.

Within a week after my first meeting with Simoni I took Bruce after work to see the property. Simoni showed us around and said the property was 24 acres with about 12 acres in grape vineyards and 10 acres in prune orchards. The price was $62,500. The vineyards were older head-pruned vines planted 8' × 8' sometime prior to 1920. The red grapes were predominately Zinfandel with scattered mixed plantings of Petite Sirah and Carignane; the white grapes were Golden Chasselas, Sauvignon Vert, and French Colombard. The prunes were sold to the Sunsweet Prune Plant in Healdsburg. The grapes were all sold to Allied Grape Growers in Asti for the Italian Swiss Colony label. There was no irrigation in either the vineyards or the orchards. Water for the residence came from a 100' well with a submersible pump that discharged about 15 gpm at low pressure. The large farmhouse, built around 1910, had 10'-high ceilings and wooden double-sash, single-pane windows. Although not ornate, the house had some nice interior moldings and paneled doors. It was a solid framed building with rough-cut clear heart redwood sided with shiplap redwood, painted white. A totally enclosed concrete cellar was directly under the house below grade; a large, covered porch wrapped around two sides of the building. There were four bedrooms, dining and living rooms, a brick fireplace, natural gas floor-furnace, kitchen, and a utility room used for laundry and auxiliary cooking. A single bathroom at ground level was under the water tower. The upper part of the tower was an empty room which had previously housed a water storage tank.[4] Wastewater and sewage went to a submerged redwood septic box with effluent discharged to an open cesspool set apart from the house.

Prior to the introduction of crawler tractors manufactured by companies like John Deere, Caterpillar, and Allis Chalmers, horses were used to tow *mold board plows* through the vineyard to turn over winter cover crops and cultivate the soil. Inside the large barn was a large inventory of prune trays and wooden lug boxes used for drying prunes and harvesting grapes, three abandoned horse stalls containing various harnesses and tack hung on a wall, a redwood fermenting tank for making wine, and a hand-cranked grape crusher and hand pump. A 1949 GMC flatbed truck was parked in the garage. A detached redwood shed contained a 1950 John Deere MC 20HP crawler tractor, various tools, lubrication equipment, shovels, and picks. Close by on the open ground was a four-section, six-foot *disc harrow* with steel drag, a wooden stand supporting a truck mount 4' × 8' steel gondola for harvesting grapes, and a gasoline hand pump with a glass bowl graduated in gallons mounted above a buried 300-gallon gasoline storage tank.

If you were looking for a typical Sonoma County farm, I suppose this might be a good example. But Bruce wasn't impressed. Compared to his father's property, which was neat, organized, and had newer buildings and better maintained younger vineyards of 100% Petite Sirah and French Colombard, the Simoni property looked run-down and in need of repair and cleanup.

Old Redwood Highway Ranch, aerial view looking northward.
Ranch house, white water tower, barn, and sheds at top center.

---

4   I later learned the tank was filled by a windmill pump and shallow well adjacent to the house that provided water to the house by gravity.

Simoni was born in Tuscany, Italy, and migrated to South America where he claimed that he was a boxer. He found his way to Sonoma County to work in the cement and plaster trades. To my knowledge, before moving into Sonoma County, he had never been married nor had he been a farmer. He acquired this property by marrying Maria Belluomini, the widow of Mateo Belluomini who had passed away at age 39 in 1952. Maria married Simoni in 1954, but she died shortly thereafter in 1957. Upon her passing, Simoni went to Italy seeking a new wife and returned with an anxious and willing partner. Together they operated the property for 14 years focused on production of prunes and grapes, but as a minimum-expense operation. Simoni never disclosed his reasons for selling the property, but it was probably due to his advancing age, and possibly because he was tired of the work. Hard frost the prior year had reduced the grape crop, and there was a possibility that vines had been damaged, which would affect future production. Also, prunes were not paying well, and Sunsweet would only buy a percentage of the delivered crop. Another factor might have been that Simoni had acquired the ranch through marriage, had operated it for only 17 years, and had never made any improvements. Probably he was not as attached to the property as were the original owners.

Bruce may have had a negative appraisal of the property, but I was thinking the opposite. Real estate in California had always been a good investment and at $2,600/acre for income-producing property with a house and farm equipment, this might be a good buy, and one I could handle if the terms were right. I was 32 years old, healthy, able, and not opposed to work. Besides my engineering job, I believed I could put in the extra effort necessary to make improvements on the property without jeopardizing my responsibilities to Ecodyne.

Another factor that made me bullish was that Sonoma County agriculture was approaching a turning point. The county at the time was widely diversified in agriculture, producing major crops of apples, hops, grapes, prunes, and vegetables. Milk, dairy, eggs, poultry, fisheries, and sheep were all major contributors to the agricultural economy. However, many of these commodities were struggling, and some farmers were working very hard to break even.

There was some progressive thinking emerging from farm advisors, educators, and winery owners based on what Napa was doing. Napa Valley, our neighbor to the east, was devoted to wine growing and had earned major national attention for their wines and vineyards. Prices for Napa grapes and wines were well above the Sonoma County averages. Sonoma County had been mainly producing red and white gallon jug wines made from field blends of undistinguished grape *varietals*, whereas Napa was producing premium wines bottled in 750 ml bottles from noble grapes: Cabernet Sauvignon, Chardonnay, and other premium varietals. Conversion of Sonoma County's prunes, apples and older generic grape vineyards to noble wine grapes for premium wines looked to be not only promising and more profitable, but also the way forward to a new future.

Jim Forchini with Carla (age 5) aboard the Johnnie Popper, 1972.

It wasn't long before I brought Anita and the kids up to see the property on a Saturday morning. We hooked up the tractor to a flatbed trailer made from the rear end axle of a Model A Ford. Anita and the kids got on, Simoni showed me how to steer the crawler tractor, and off we went for a ride around the property going between vineyard avenues and orchards while chasing out jack rabbits along the way. The sky was clear and bright, the air had an invigorating freshness, and the popping sound of the tractor chugging through the vineyard was comparable to a model train ride in a theme park.[5] The kids loved it. And I could see Anita was starting to open her mind towards the possibilities of living on a farm. When we returned to the yard, Anita gave the old farmhouse a good look over, clearly pondering whether this large old farmhouse could be spruced up to provide some charm and comfort.

My mind was made up. I wanted to buy the Simoni ranch, but Anita was slow to come to any decision. I lobbied Bruce to talk to Anita and encourage her about the benefits

---

5   John Deere Model M tractors were commonly referred to by the local growers as "Johnnie Poppers." This was because the low rpm, high-torque 2 cylinder engine with its huge fly wheel (which maintained rotational inertia) made a loud pop-pop-pop sound as the large pistons cycled through four strokes of internal combustion.

of raising grapes and the healthy agrarian lifestyle it would provide. Anita was friendly with Bruce's wife, Joan, and realized Joan was a happy housewife raising four kids and growing commercial Halloween pumpkins on the side to go with Bruce's part-time grape growing and work at Ecodyne. Anita started to think the old Simoni farmhouse might be a good place to showcase all the antique furniture she had been starting to acquire and refurbish. She thought about how our kids would have a safe, open place to play, and the opportunities to raise some animals, join 4H, and develop an appreciation for the outdoor environment. After two months of deliberation, Anita agreed to go along with me, and we decided that if we could come to terms with Simoni, we should buy the place. I had my salary and benefits from Ecodyne, some bank savings and some appreciated common stock from my tenure with JPL, all of which could be used for down payment. We wouldn't be solely dependent upon any grape income to make ends meet. The more we thought about it, the more we came to the same conclusion . . . ***let's do it!***

Making An Offer, Closing the Deal

On a weekend in early December 1970, I had brought my father up to see the Simoni property. My father spoke fluent Italian, and, after I introduced him to Simoni and showed him the property and all the equipment, a conversation in Italian developed off to the side between my father and Simoni. I couldn't fully understand what was being said. Afterwards my father told me there was a problem with the sale because Simoni had given exclusive rights to sell his property to three different Italian realtors: named Scalione, Barbieri, and Giovannoni. Whether Simoni was just ignorant of the terms of these sale agreements or whether he just played by his own rules wasn't clear. I later learned that Simoni had a reputation for being ornery. He was not on good terms with his immediate neighbors and did not have many friends in the community. He had told me not to talk with the neighbors or anyone concerning a potential sale to me.

When the three realtors heard about Simoni's intended direct sale to me, and the independent listings for all three of them, they were furious and threatened legal action against Simoni. To resolve the chaos, Simoni engaged a local man by the name of Catalani to act as a go-between in negotiating a settlement with the three realtors and allow Simoni to deal directly with me. Catalani was from Tuscany and worked at a local company that fabricated wine crushers and pumps. A superb mechanic who also had a real estate license, he was a pleasant man with lots of friends in the community. He was a good choice to be a mediator. While the entire fiasco was beginning to take on the appearance of a Type B Italian movie, it was finally settled by Catalani with agreeable terms between the parties. I later learned one of the realtors settled for $125, but I never found out what settlements were made to the other two, or if Catalani was ever compensated. Simoni, however, now wanted to up the price from $62,500 to $65,000, which I assumed might have had something to do with his settlement agreements. Anita and I pondered the increase in sales price but finally decided it was still a good investment, and we made an offer to Simoni to purchase the ranch in an "as is" condition with all equipment included.

Our offer was a $20,000 down payment with Simoni carrying a note for $45,000 at 7% interest secured by a 1st deed of trust, and with an annual payment including interest of $6,407, and a final balloon payment in 10 years for any unpaid balance. In addition, we agreed to let Simoni live in the house rent-free as property caretaker, which would include hiring and supervising vineyard workers as needed for vineyard operation. All labor, supplies, and chemical expenses would be paid by me. I would do the tractor work and use my vacation for harvest. In addition, Simoni was to teach me in the various practices that he employed as a grower and assist me when I needed help. He accepted our offer and agreed to the terms and conditions we had set forth, although nothing was in writing except the terms of the $45,000 note. His word to me on what equipment was included in the ranch sale, and his willingness to oversee and help out on the property in exchange for rent, was good enough for me. My thoughts were that it was better to take an older man's word versus a formal written document that might have negated a sale. This naive assumption on my part would come back to haunt me.

Simoni had one other condition on terms. He told me not to talk to either the neighboring couple who lived in the white house next to our driveway, or to the couple in the green house, down the private road. I never asked why, and at the time it was of no immediate concern to me. The fact that he was holding the note on the property, that I was using him as caretaker, and that I would be working with him, meant I was going to honor his request.

On January 7, 1971, we entered escrow independent of any real estate agent, and on February 7, 1971, Anita and I became the owners of the Simoni property. I was excited to be the new owner of the property, and I felt very fortunate. There were other locals in the community who had expressed an interest in buying Simoni's property, but because of his temperament and his vengeance toward neighbors and others, I reckoned he sold to me, an outsider, out of spite. I also believed that he sold to me because he really thought I would fall on my face, would find the work too difficult, and I would default on payments, and he would get the ranch back.

Balancing a Change in Lifestyle

Over a period of three years of my employment at Ecodyne from 1967 through 1970, Don, Sam, and I had completed designs and drawings for most of the new products, and we were ready to subcontract procurement or supervise in-house fabrication. Over that period my salary as a Project Engineer had increased 20%. In December 1970, at about the same time I purchased the Simoni property, Sam was transferred to the Erection Department, and I was promoted to become Manager of New Product Development (NPD). My salary would increase by 10%. I was thrilled to get this promotion, and the salary boost would help with my operational expenses for the vineyard. As manager of NPD, I would report to the Vice President of Engineering and supervise three project engineers. I would finish the design of some smaller projects involving pipe seals, pipe valves, distribution boxes, and nozzles. I would maintain liaison with vendors and suppliers relating to the new products.

Ecodyne was my bread-and-butter job, Monday to Friday. But I stayed in communication with Simoni to stay abreast of operations on the vineyard, and on Saturdays I was eager to put on the jeans and take the kids up to the ranch to walk around, take a tractor ride, and do some work in the vineyard. In addition to what I learned from Simoni and Bruce, I studied the techniques of pruning, training vines, and vineyard development, relying on pamphlets from UC Davis Viticultural Department that were readily available from the Sonoma County Farm Advisor. I also purchased the book *General Viticulture* (1962) by UC Davis professor A.J. Winkler, and I read and studied every chapter thoroughly. I also attended a seminar presented by wine industry leaders and farm educators in which local growers were encouraged to remove prunes and older generic vineyards and to replant with premium varietal wine grapes. When I asked Simoni if he might like to go with me as a matter of interest, his attitude was indignant and he retorted, "Do you want me to go as the student or the teacher."

Even though escrow hadn't closed, time was wasting, and Simoni got me started quickly in late January by hiring three Mexican workers for the pruning: Asencion, Tony, and Juan. Juan only had one arm, but he assured me he could keep up with the rest. He was right.

I learned the basics of pruning head-pruned vines. It was important to have the vine's arms well-spaced and the head of the vine open to allow sun to penetrate the vine. The vines had to be compact to allow cross cultivation by tractor. I enjoyed pruning, and I would prune for 3-4 hours on Saturday mornings whenever possible. My first pruning payroll was $41 for 24 manhours ($1.70/hr.). The entire cost of pruning, not counting my involvement, ended up being $429. In addition to the pruning expense, I had winter expenses for vine replants, stakes, fertilizer, gasoline, lubricants, and workers' compensation insurance.

In February, my maternal grandparents came up from Bakersfield to see the vineyard. I was anxious to show my Nonno Pietro the property because of his love for the vine, his contadino history as a young boy in Italy, and his winemaking experience with Paso Robles Zinfandel grapes. I thought he would be eager to see what I had acquired, and he was. As we walked the vineyard, I described the little I had learned about the property.

Pietro (Nonno) Bernacchi at left, Jim Forchini at right.
Old Redwood Highway Ranch, 1971.

There was no comparison in personalities and character between Simoni and my grandfather Pietro. Simoni could at times be mean, crude, and ill-mannered, whereas my grandfather was soft spoken, mild, and gentle. Regardless of these differences in character, they engaged and spoke in Italian. Although I couldn't comprehend the entire conversation, I observed Simoni doing most of the talking, trying to impress my grandfather, while Nonno Pietro silently listened and gave an occasional smile. After this brief visit, I felt my grandfather was proud of what I had done. He was happy that family genes were in play and that continuation of winegrowing was being carried on to a new generation.

By the end of February, Simoni and I had burned all the brush from pruning in a steel-sided sled pulled by tractor down vineyard roads that separated the various blocks of grapes. The brush was pitch-forked into the sled and the ash fell to the ground through slots in the sled bottom. It was hard work picking up multiple piles of entangled canes to lift over the 4'-high sled siding. After completing the burn, Simoni taught me how to tie vines to supporting stakes. There was a stub of a willow tree on the property that was heavily pruned in pollard fashion to produce multiple slender canes. The canes were around 3' in length, very limber and flexible, and could be bent and wrapped around the trunk of a vine to secure to a stake. The technique of securing the willow wrap in place was unique and involved a particular twist and tuck to secure the tie from unwrapping. This was a renewable source of tie material preferred by most of the Italian growers, and it was common practice to find on vineyard property a willow tree pruned severely to produce such ties. Willow ties were an alternative to raffia twine, but they would eventually be replaced by plastic tape and interlocking chain and aluminum bands.

Later that month we borrowed a fertilizer spreader from a grower in Dry Creek. It was a homemade spreader that used a Maytag washer tub to hold and spread ammonia nitrate granules. The spreader was mounted on the rear axle of a Model A Ford truck, and the truck wheels drove the differential gearbox, which drove the agitator shaft in the tub which cast the fertilizer outward about 16'. The sacks of fertilizer were stacked on the spreader, and one of us fed the spreader tub while the other drove the tractor.

Later that month, for $22.50, I joined the North Coast Grape Growers Association (NCGGA), which was an association of growers from Napa, Sonoma, and Mendocino counties, thinking I might further my knowledge of grape growing by associating with some full-time grape growers. It was thoroughly enjoyable meeting and associating with these experienced growers, many of whom were older with a lot of stories to tell. I found the members not only interesting, but also decent, down-to-earth people from whom I could learn a lot. An additional benefit of this growers' organization was the huge annual dinner meeting at Lena's Italian Restaurant in Santa Rosa. Numerous bottles of various North Coast wines were set out on the table every four feet, to be enjoyed with generous plates of salami, cheese, salad, hearty pasta, and roast beef. I was starting to become totally mesmerized by being a part-time grape grower.

In early April, Simoni taught me how to cultivate the vineyard using the John Deere tractor with the four-section *disc harrow*. The disc-cutting angle was set by pulling from a rope that was attached to a lever while sitting on the tractor seat. The lever actuated a pawl and locking rack on the disc, and when the tractor was moved slowly forward, the disc would move to an angle that would result in the desired cut. When exiting a vine row and making a tight turn, a reverse operation was necessary: the tractor was moved in reverse to unlock the rack, allowing the disc-cutting angle to return to straight position. This process took a lot of time before entering and exiting a vineyard row.

The non-trellis vineyard was planted 8' × 8', which allowed cross cultivation to eliminate the winter cover crop of weeds and grasses. Cross cultivation would be required two to three times a year to develop a weed-free tillage of loose soil that would conserve moisture for the non-irrigated vineyard. Concurrent with cultivation, two men were hired to hoe and sucker around the vines, which took 96 man-hours. After spring bud break, two neighboring growers were hired to dust the vineyard using sulfur backpacks at a cost of $44 for each treatment. The men would hand pump the bellows on the backpack that would blow the sulfur into the center of the vine through a hose fitted with a diffuser. This process was necessary to control powdery mildew on the grapes that could develop under humid weather conditions.

Although I hadn't yet had the experience of a harvest, I had now basically completed Grape Growing 101. The rest was going to be up to me by learning by doing, studying Winkler, talking with Bruce, and learning from other growers within the NCGGA. I was now a part-time grape grower, and I needed to find a way to balance between my engineering job responsibilities at Ecodyne, my family, and my new involvement with the vineyard.

Collision Course

Six months into ownership and operation of the vineyard, my relationship with Simoni began to falter. Simoni clearly started to regret his sale to me; his temperament changed, and he became difficult to deal with. I believed the reason was that property values were increasing, and that he began thinking maybe he had sold prematurely and at too low a price. Grape growers were being advised by influential industry advisors to remove prunes and older generic vineyards and to replant with premium varietal grapes. Napa Valley was a beacon for all to see; Napa grape growers were receiving good prices for Cabernet, Chardonnay, Sauvignon Blanc, and other noble grape varieties. Bank of America had recently published a bullish report on the potential in growing premium varietal grapes in Sonoma County, and the bank was lending money for vineyard development. There was optimism that Sonoma County would enjoy the same benefits as Napa, by conversion from prunes, hops, vegetables, and apples to premium varietal grapes. There were increased prospects for higher profitability for grape growers, and escalation in values of property suitable for vineyard planting.

Simoni told me in July that his doctor had advised him not to work anymore, and for this reason he wasn't going to do any more physical work as we had agreed upon. But he looked good to me, and he behaved the same without any noticeable signs of physical impairment or symptoms of failing health. Without the benefit of a letter from his doctor, my immediate thought was he was not being truthful. For some reason, he believed his alleged failing health gave him the right to live in the house as caretaker even though he was unable to work. He soon gave away the wine making equipment in the barn without my knowledge, and then he advised he would be selling the farm equipment. On one occasion, I saw him filling his car with gasoline I had purchased for the vineyards, whereupon I told him that was never allowed in the past and was not to be done now. His previous experience as a pugnacious boxer was starting to show, and I thought he was trying to challenge me hoping I might falter.

The final blow came when he advised I could not remove any prunes until the $45,000 balance on the note was paid off entirely. I realized right away I was in trouble, but I could only blame myself for having nothing in writing concerning our agreement, only the terms of payment on the promissory note. I did remind him that three realtors were all aware of the equipment included in the ranch sale, and that my father and Catalani were witness to the terms and conditions that allowed Simoni to live on the ranch as caretaker. He did seem nervously concerned about this fact, which gave me some faint hope he might be bluffing on selling the equipment. I didn't care about the old wine equipment being given away since I had no intention of using it, but I did care about the truck, harvest gondola, tractor, and cultivation equipment. And I did want to remove the prunes.

To avoid any expense for an attorney or any argument with an old man who wasn't trustworthy, I decided I needed to pay Simoni the $45,000 balance due on the note in order to remove the prunes that year after harvest. I did not have the funds to pay the loan in full, and I would have to find a lender quickly. I told Simoni it was my intent to remove the prunes after harvest, and I would seek funding to pay him off entirely as quickly as possible. I also told him he would be asked to leave the property after he was paid off. That set him back a bit. I thought he believed we would never come up with the money, that we would give this whole thing up of being a grape grower, and he'd get the ranch back and stay in the house. He didn't know me very well!

Anita and I now had to prepare ourselves to sell our country home and move onto the ranch to manage and operate the property. I didn't want to look for a new caretaker or be an absentee owner anymore. Considering the redevelopment vineyard work I that had planned, it was best we live on the property. Besides, I felt Anita and the kids would love it. With that in mind, we advertised our Santa Rosa home "For Sale By Owner". The house quickly sold at a nice gain after our four years of ownership. However, it was necessary to make an interim move to a 2-bedroom duplex in a northern suburb of Santa Rosa. We sadly terminated our swim club membership at Oakpark where we had spent so many enjoyable times. But we kept our Sierra cabin at Pinecrest, which we planned to continue using, although perhaps less frequently.

Concurrent with all the discourse, stress, and distraction that had occurred with Simoni, I was deeply involved and committed to my work at Ecodyne as the new manager of New Product Development. There remained some design work on some smaller products, and there was travel to jobsites to handle situations with installation and startup of the gearboxes and fan assemblies. I couldn't let the problems that had developed with Simoni interfere with my full-time salaried job. As a father and husband, I also had to make time for family. It was a challenge to be juggling all these responsibilities, but I was determined to make it work. After all, this was my idea.

Now on my mind were the prunes and how they added to the burden and extra operations expense. They would need to be harvested in August without the help of Simoni. I had no interest in prunes, knowing the plan was to remove them after harvest in preparation of planting vineyard. Without Simoni guidance on the prune harvest, I needed help. I was lucky to find a neighbor named Ponzo, who was an established prune grower connected to the Sunsweet Cooperative. He agreed to pay me $100 to take over the prune crop, plus he would get all the income from the crop. I was quick to accept his offer because everything I had heard about prunes indicated they were a losing proposition, and growers worked hard to break even, or they even lost money. Maybe I sold short, but taking care of a prune orchard and harvesting prunes was one less thing I had to worry about, and that made life easier.

In August while attending a grower's seminar in Santa Rosa, I met a representative from Equitable Life Assurance who was making loans for vineyard development. I needed a loan to pay off Simoni and made an application to borrow $40,000. With that loan plus an additional $5,000 from my savings, I could pay off the Simoni note. On September 10, 1971, Equitable approved my loan (20-year term, at 8.5% annual interest, $2,000 annual payments) with the provision that Simoni would terminate the promissory note agreement between us and relinquish his rights and possession of the property, effective September 1, 1971. At that point Simoni realized I was not going to give up my determination to be a grape grower, and on September 28 he signed an agreement for Equitable's stipulations. He purchased a small house in town and moved off the property in late October, and with that, my relationship with him ended.

I was relieved the matter had been resolved, but I was somewhat saddened because Simoni, in spite of his faults, had given me my start and helped me at the beginning. In 1971 I was an "early outsider," and Healdsburg was a very tightly knit population of multi-generational local families and farmers. Outsiders were not well received by some locals. Outsiders were looked at as intruders in this closed community. Several locals had wanted the Simoni property, but he sold to me because of his temperament, difficult relationships with others, and probably out of spite. I was grateful to be able to purchase the property, but at the same time I felt a little guilty that Simoni had favored me instead of selling to other, possibly more deserving, local growers.

Simoni was one of the first of established locals to sell to early outsiders entering Healdsburg with the goal of entering the wine industry. Other early outsiders from other professions who entered during the time frame 1962-1975, and who had no winegrowing experience, but a strong desire to get involved in the wine industry and become winegrowers, were:

- Rodney Strong, Windsor Vineyard, Professional Dancer

- Leo Trentadue, Trentadue Winery, Bay Area retail Business Owner

- Harry Wetzel, Alexander Valley Vineyards, Aircraft Executive

- Tim Murphy, Murphy-Goode Winery, Retail Food, Business Owner

- Russ Green, Simi Winery, former Signal Oil & Gas Executive

- Dave Stare, Dry Creek Vineyards, Railroad Engineering Executive

- Lou Preston, Preston Winery, MBA, Business and Accounting

As of this writing, the top five names on this list have passed on. Russ Green had sold his Simi Winery, but his Hoot Owl Vineyards are still in operation by his family. Dave Stare retired and turned over the operation of his winery and vineyards to his daughter. Lou Preston is still very active today operating Preston Vineyards & Winery.

Another group of early outsiders without agricultural experience followed me, entering between 1972-1976 as part-time grape growers in different AVA locations. They were among my close friends from Ecodyne:

- Gordon Wistrom, Thermal Engineer, Dry Creek Valley

- Claude Potts, Repair Sales, Dry Creek Valley

- Robert Stone, Structural Engineer, Russian River Valley

- Ray Osenga, Quality Control Engineer, Dry Creek Valley

- Dick Simon, Marketing, Redwood Valley, Mendocino County

I don't know whether they were influenced by my transition and involvement as a part time grower, by my friend and part-time grower Bruce, or by their own self-developed interest. They were smitten like me, and they took advantage of what appeared to be promising opportunities in the Sonoma County wine industry. None of them are still operating as wine grape growers. Gordon Wistrom lasted for over 40 years as an active grower and was very successful.

I could understand Simoni's regret in selling the ranch, and his realization that he was finished as a farmer, entering retirement. In retrospect, he probably agonized over the thought that maybe he could have received a higher price had he waited. At the beginning he thought he was doing the right thing by selling to me for $65,000. Ultimately, I believed he had concluded that his life as a grape grower was getting harder and was coming to an end, that he was getting on in age, that his son was not interested in carrying on the farm, and that his property needed a lot of work. After moving into town, Simoni never returned to the ranch, and I never saw him again. He died the following year of a heart attack while climbing a bluff on the Sonoma Coast while fishing for abalone.

First Harvest

As the 1971 grape harvest came upon us, we were not ready to move onto the ranch because Simoni was still in the house, and he had until November 1st to vacate. The prunes had been harvested by Ponzo in August without incident or any involvement on my part, but now grape harvest was fast approaching. I was wondering how I would handle this harvest without Simoni's guidance. At Simoni's request I had kept my distance from the grape-growing neighbors who bordered my property. I had ignored them for six months, and I didn't feel right imposing upon them for advice. Bruce had no experience harvesting old head pruned vines planted at 8' spacing. His vineyard had 12' spacing, and he could go between rows with a gondola and bins. My old vines spaced at 8' were an entanglement of canes that created a jangled, intertwining maze of snares. Picking this vineyard was very difficult, and there was risk of damaging canes and fruit.

Somehow the word got out by the local underground that I was in a dilemma. At the time, I didn't realize I was being silently observed by the surrounding community. A nearby grower from Limerick Lane by the name of Andrew Sodini, whom I didn't know, responded to a plea from my guardian angel that I needed help. Sodini was an older man in his late 60s, well mannered, soft-spoken like my grandfather Pietro, and neat in appearance. He was a long-time grape grower who had had a small winery at one time producing bulk wine for resale. Like Simoni, he also sold his grapes to Allied Grape Growers in Asti. Sodini was not particularly fond of Simoni, but he knew him well. At times they shared use of the brush burning sled, and he was familiar with the way Simoni handled his grape harvest. Sodini came down the hill on a bright Saturday morning in mid-September to introduce himself. He asked if I needed help. He was willing to be of assistance and help me get started if I wanted. Absolutely, I wanted his help. . . . Not only did I want his help, but I needed him. I embraced him with open arms. Sodini was the epitome of the decent, older growers I had met at CNCGGA.

Sodini told me he knew of a family in Forestville who could come to do the picking, and that he could arrange it. I was grateful because my Spanish vocabulary was very limited. I had taken Spanish as my foreign language in high school for college prep, but I had not used it since. I realized I needed to brush up quickly with the numbers, words, and commands I might need for harvest.

Sodini advised I needed to get about 200 wooden lug boxes from the barn and examine their condition. The boxes would have to be cleaned by hosing with water to remove mold, cobwebs, varmint excrement, and insects. They needed to be nailed securely and in good shape because they would be used to hold about 50 pounds of grapes.

He showed me how to lay out the picking procedure for the rows spaced at 8 feet where the vines of the row were also spaced at 8'.[6] Using pruning shears, avenues would be cut every 16 rows to allow my John Deere tractor to enter the avenue with a narrow trailer. Entangled canes of each vine would be snipped so the pickers could move freely without breaking canes connected to the vine spurs that would produce next year's crop. Empty lug boxes would be spaced on the sides of the avenues. Pickers would be assigned an identification number. Each picker would commence picking eight vines out from the avenue on the first row, working towards the avenue. When the vines of that row were picked, the picker would start the next row eight vines out, and work inward toward the avenue. The pickers were never to be allowed to start on the first vine in the row and work outwards towards the middle, because they were apt to leave unpicked vines. Once a lug was filled, the picker would mark his number with chalk on the side of the lug, and then place the lug on the avenue for pick up and tabulation by the same tractor/trailer that had set them out empty. When the tractor had a full load of 32 grape lugs, it would pull up alongside a flatbed truck with a gondola and two men would dump the lugs until about 200 lugs filled a 5-ton gondola.

First harvest, loading lugs onto the flatbed truck, 1971.

---

6   This procedure was for a vineyard where the vines were equally spaced at 8'. Rows of vines were also spaced at 8', forming cross rows.

When the gondola was full, I would drive the flatbed truck off to the winery for delivery, hoping everything would go well in the vineyard during my absence. Having no field boss, I could only hope everyone would stay busy, leave no grapes on the vine, or leave a vine unpicked. The pickers were paid by the box, which meant they would pick fast and sometimes not pick clean, resulting in grapes or vines being left behind. When I was present, I was always walking the rows behind the pickers, ensuring everything was properly harvested. I always hated to leave the vineyard to deliver grapes because it could amount to a long period away, and if the winery was busy or had a mechanical breakdown, I could be gone for over two hours.

Basically, that was the harvest procedure. We would start at around 7:00 am and stop around 2:00 pm. Assuming there were no labor problems, adverse weather, mechanical problems, or delays and holds placed by the winery, we could finish harvest in about one week.

I did not want to be a co-op grower with Allied Grape Growers because I had no faith the old '49 GMC truck could make the 16-mile round trips to Asti without some mishap. Another factor was that AGG only owned 18% of Asti, having sold 82% of their holdings in 1968 to Heublein, a major distillery and vodka producer. This didn't sit well with me. They were not local wine people but rather a large national corporation.

On Sodini's recommendation, I connected with Eugene "Pete" Seghesio of Seghesio Winery in Healdsburg. Pete was the son of Eduardo Seghesio, one of the original owners of Asti's Italian Swiss Colony between 1919-1920. Pete had a wealth of experience in both grape growing and wine making. He came to look at the vineyard on a Saturday morning and we walked the ranch together inspecting the various blocks of vines. I pointed out to him the different blocks of red and white grape varietals that I had acquired with the Simoni property. Seghesio was quick to correct me on my mistakes in identity of varietals. He would describe in detail how to identify the different varietals from the leaves, berry size, cluster characteristics, and color of the berry. I was learning from the master. He was the teacher. . . . I was the student and all ears.

Seghesio liked what he saw, and he wanted the grapes. He said they would be purchased as Red Zinfandel and Mixed White, and the price would be determined similar to that of a co-op. That is, the bulk wine produced would be sold on the open market at the best possible price, and after deducting production expenses, the growers would be paid equally a net $/ton based on the tons they delivered. At that time Seghesio did not produce a branded wine with the Seghesio name on the label. On an annual basis, they would purchase and crush about 5,000 tons of grapes from local growers, producing a million gallons of wine. While the many growers who delivered grapes to Seghesio on a regular yearly basis were considered "Seghesio growers," there was no written contract executed between a grower and the Seghesio winery. On a hand shake I fell in line with the growers before me to deliver my first harvest to Seghesio Winery. I was proud to be accepted by Seghesio as one of their growers. Their winery was highly regarded.

Harvest began on September 21ˢᵗ, and I used one week of my two-week vacation to be in the vineyard managing the operation. Simoni was still on the property but offered no assistance. He watched from a distance, and I thought maybe he was waiting for me to have problems or a breakdown that so often might occur during a harvest. The drive to the Seghesio winery was about three miles, which in my mind was about the maximum distance the old truck could safely travel without mishap. I had no experience using this truck under a heavy load, and I worried about mechanical breakdown, dead battery, starting problems, or brake failure. I would be learning a lot about its condition, but fortunately I escaped all those perils on this first harvest, although I did discover the radiator would leak, and it was necessary to carry water in a jug to prevent overheating, or I would never make it back home.

The family of 10 from Forestville, who had been arranged by Sodini, were a mix of hard-working men and women, young and old, and everyone got along well. Pickers were paid 50 cents a lug. Two boys helped me cut the avenues for picking, pick up the lugs in the vineyard, tally the boxed grapes and load the gondola. They were not required to pick and were paid $1.65/hour.

At the winery, my truck loaded with grapes in the gondola would be weighed on a platform scale, and a sample of the grapes would be tested for sugar by an independent, non-winery-related third party. The procedure involved inserting a 4" metal tube deep into the *gondola* in several places to get a representative sample. The sample would be crushed with a small roller crusher and the juice measured for sugar content (Brix) using a refractometer. If the juice met minimum requirements, the truck could proceed to the crush stand. The gondola was hinged on one side. When the truck was positioned alongside a long metal hopper containing a large screw conveyor, the gondola would be rotated by a hoist on an overhead beam, the grapes would empty into the hopper, and the conveyor would convey the grapes to the crusher. When the gondola was emptied, the truck would return to the weigh station to be weighed out. I was provided a receipt showing the date, grape *variety*, and net tons delivered.

That was the way it was intended to work although on occasion there would be a mechanical problem with equipment causing delays, and the line would back up to the crusher. When these things happened, Seghesio would offer a glass of wine with a snack in the cellar storage room as I waited. These delays also provided opportunities to talk with other growers who were also delayed, to discuss how well or poorly the harvest was going.

By September 28th we had completed the harvest and had picked 51.2 tons of grapes of which 40.8 tons of mixed reds sold as Zinfandel and 10.4 tons of mixed white grapes (Colombard, Chasselas, and Sauvignon Vert). These tonnages were net after 10-15% loss because of shrivel caused by four days of extreme temperatures in September (104°F, 109°F, 113°F, and 114°F). In early December that year, I received payment by mail for the 1971 harvest. I eagerly opened the envelope like a kid opening Christmas presents to discover what prices Segehsio had paid for the grapes. To my delight $350/ton was paid for the Zinfandel and $250/ton for the mixed whites. An additional $10/ton was paid on both varieties for hauling. My total crop income was $17,398 and my harvest expense was $1,454. At the end of 1971 my total ranch expenses were $10,527 and, including the $100 I received from Ponzo for the prunes, my net profit for my first year was $6,971. Not too bad for a little part-time effort!

Bruce was right about picking up some extra money as a part-time grape grower. But he was wrong on his negative appraisal of the Simoni property that had earned me a nifty 66% profit!

In November after the 1971 harvest, I engaged a local heavy equipment operator to remove all the prunes growing on the property. He used a D7 Cat tractor to bulldoze the trees from the ground and dig out as many roots as possible. This operation was followed by hand picking residual broken roots from the holes. The trees and roots were piled for burning after drying. The next operation before planting was to deep-rip the soil, 3' deep in three directions, to break any hardpan that had developed over the years from cultivation and compaction.

Getting Established Wearing Two Hats

In November 1971, Simoni left the property, and the grape harvest was finished. It was time to move from our two-bedroom duplex to the ranch. Anita and I with the two kids moved onto the property before Thanksgiving and began adjusting to living in an old farmhouse. Anita and I took the larger bedroom, which had a huge double-sash, single-pane window overlooking our north sloping vineyards. Carla and Mike each had a large bedroom with a single window looking west over the vineyards. The fourth and smallest bedroom was converted to my office and library. With the exception of our master bedroom, you could walk through arched doorways directly through Carla's bedroom, Mike's bedroom, and my office. The single bathroom was on the south side of the house. To reach it, It was necessary to walk through the arched openings connecting the living room, dining room, kitchen, and laundry room. The bathroom had no heat, but the living room was heated by a natural gas floor furnace, and the dining room had a brick fireplace. The kitchen had only two electrical outlets, one for the refrigerator and the other for small appliances on the kitchen countertop. There was no dishwasher or electric garbage disposal. There was a natural gas supply for a stove, and the laundry room also had natural gas service and enough space to install a dryer and washing machine. Concrete steps led underneath the house to a large 12' × 16' cellar with standing head room. A crude shower head supplied some water in the cellar, and the water simply drained to a perforated pipe underground. The farmhouse wasn't the modern home we had enjoyed in Santa Rosa with central heating, two bathrooms, and built-in electrical appliances. But it was our home now, and we were determined to fix it up, make it comfortable, and enjoy the vineyards, environment, and our new life on the ranch.

Old Redwood Highway Ranch farmhouse. Michael and Carla Forchini at left, ca. 1972.

No sooner had we moved in, when travel responsibilities at Ecodyne started to emerge. In 1972, I flew to the island of Borneo for 10 days to solve a persistent fan blade erosion problem at a liquid nitrogen plant. After that, I was sent to Alberta, Canada, in the middle of winter, when a fan blade broke and went through the fan stack. I then travelled to Texas to monitor the fabrication of our gearbox castings and gears, and to Ecodyne's newly acquired fabrication plant in Tulsa, Oklahoma, where fan blades, hubs, and motor and gear supports were fabricated and gearboxes were assembled. By the end of the year, my department had completed the final designs on the valves, seals, and nozzles of the cooling tower components that Ecodyne was developing. My focus now was following progress on procurement, fabrication, installation, and startup of all the new products that had been developed since 1967. I had many meetings with Don, and I also met with the Marketing Dept. on a regular basis, to keep everyone informed on the startup and performance of new cooling towers using our new products.

During my absences from our ranch, I felt bad having to leave Anita alone with the kids with no close contacts except the immediate neighbors, whom we had never met. Now that Simoni had been paid off and was gone from the property, I was anxious to forget any commitment I had made to him about not talking with the neighbors. It was time to get acquainted. On a bright sunny Saturday in April, I was busy laying out and pounding stakes for a new one-acre Zinfandel block that had been previously in prunes. After lunch I took a break and wandered about the yard soaking up the sun and giving my aching body a rest. Across the road I noticed an older man working in the vineyard near the road. When he saw me, he stood up and in tone of frustration shouted, "What's a matter with you . . . ? You no talk to me?" I was embarrassed. I had been ignoring my neighbor for too long since Simoni left. I walked over to him, shook his hand and apologized for being so rude and explained that I had only been following Simoni's wishes. He laughed. He knew exactly the situation.

Arnold (Arnie) Bruschera holding godson Andrew Forchini, ca. 1977.

The older man's name was Arnold Bruschera. He was from Lombardy, Italy, the same region as my paternal grandfather. His scolding and stern look soon turned to a warm smile showing that he was happy I had crossed over the road to introduce myself. I guessed he was in his late 60s. He was clean and neatly dressed in khakis and sweater, and he had a gentle manner about him. I judged he was decent man of good character.

Bruschera lived with his wife, Jennie, in the small white house adjacent to our property. They had no children. He farmed about 20 acres of older mixed red vines and did all the work himself, including pruning and tractor cultivation. He sold his grapes to Allied Grape Growers making many round trips to Asti in his 1-ton Dodge flatbed truck fitted with a 2-ton gondola. After a brief conversation he was anxious to know if I would like to taste his wine, to which I replied, "Sure . . . I'd love to." He invited me into his cellar for a glass of his home-made Zinfandel blend. It was strong in alcohol, dark in color, heavy in structure, and tannic. It reminded me of my grandfather Pietro's wine.

After two glasses of his wine, I was feeling high, rejuvenated, and in an elated mood. I went home to tell Anita I had met our immediate neighbor, who was unbelievably nice. The combination of his potent wine and my jubilation led to the suggestion we should celebrate our upcoming anniversary at the Healdsburg House, a recently opened Italian restaurant located close by. We sought out Ponzo, the man who had harvested the prunes. Ponzo had a teenage daughter whom we recruited to watch the kids. I dressed up in a sport coat and tie, Anita wore a fancy dress, and we kicked up our heels and went out for dinner. This event led to an unforgettable episode as a young winegrower in Healdsburg.

Healdsburg House was an older estate home, surrounded by prune orchards, that had been converted to a restaurant. The house was close in age to our farmhouse but had fancier interior moldings and furnishings. It was obviously the home of a successful person, who I surmised might have been the owner of the adjacent orchards. The restaurant had a warm comfortable feeling inside, and was filled to capacity. A table wasn't immediately available, so we ordered two Manhattan cocktails and waited in the bar until called. For dinner, we both ordered prime rib along with a bottle of Pinot Noir. After consuming all the wine and finishing a large and delicious dinner. Anita lit up a Salem menthol cigarette. Although I was an addicted pipe smoker at the time, I decided to join her by smoking one of her cigarettes to celebrate a wonderful meal and day; but after a few puffs on the cigarette, I felt totally dizzy, blacked out, and fell over in my chair. Seated at an adjacent table was a man, who happened to be a candidate running for the school board, and his wife, who happened to be a nurse. She immediately laid me out on the floor, loosened my collar and tie, massaged my chest, and called for an ambulance thinking I had had a heart attack. When I came to, the medics were carrying me out the door on a stretcher headed to Healdsburg Hospital. I tried in vain to tell them I was OK, and shouted out to Anita to pay the check. But they disregarded my plea and took me to the hospital. At the hospital, they wired me for an EKG and monitored my heart for a couple of hours, and then insisted I spend the night as an extra precaution. I argued that I felt fine and wanted to go home. I simply believed I had been overcome by a strenuous physical day of pounding stakes in the vineyard coupled with Arnold's overpowering wine, the Manhattan cocktail, the bottle of Pinot, and the unaccustomed cigarette. All this had resulted in a tired and intoxicated body that was sure to pass out at any moment. The bewildered ER staff finally gave up and agreed to let me go home. Before I left, the woman who was a nurse and who initially attended to me in the restaurant, stopped by the hospital to see if I was OK. She asked if she could release a statement. In my fatigued state, not knowing what she meant, I said sure. The next day, buried in the paper under local news, I spotted a headline . . . "Candidate's Wife Saves Stricken Diner." On Monday morning, I was back at work at Ecodyne explaining to friends and employees that it was nothing, I was fine. But the episode was certainly a lesson in moderation.

Back at the ranch, I sought to meet our other neighbor, Larry Biagi, who lived in the small green house at the entrance road to our property. Biagi and his partner, Bellagio, built redwood storage tanks and wine fermenters in a small plant that was the former Sodini Winey on Limerick Lane. Biagi farmed two acres of older grapes. He lived with his wife, Nancy, and they had two older children who lived close by. He was in his late 50s. He was very personable, liked to talk endlessly, and was curious about everything I was doing. I couldn't drive down the road without him seeing me coming. He would wave me down so he could talk and ask what I was up to. Both Bruschera and Biagi were wonderful neighbors who took a great interest in our family, loved our kids, and made us feel very comfortable in our new home.

After making friends with neighbors Bruschera and Biagi, I felt more at ease about work-related travel. I was going to have more travel to Texas to monitor the fabrication of our gearbox castings and gears, and to Oklahoma where gearboxes would be assembled and fan blades, hubs, and motor and gear supports fabricated. I was thankful that Anita could call on our neighbors for assistance, if needed, when I was away, and that she would be in very good hands.

Rainfall had been below normal during December of 1971, and January was also dry. By the end of January, I had completed pruning, burned all the brush, and fertilized the vineyard. My labor costs went to $2.25/hr. The weather in February of 1972 was unseasonably warm, and in late March we had six days of frost. In April, I planted four acres of Pinot Noir and Zinfandel in areas that had formerly been prunes. In July, we had four days of triple-digit extreme heat with temperatures as high as 117°F. We harvested between September 30 and October 9. The weather abnormities of low rainfall, frost, and heat resulted in a drop in production of 54% from the previous year. Our 23.8 tons of delivered grapes yielded an income of $11,946, down 32% from last year. Fortunately, this much lower yield was partly offset by average price increases of 43% on the reds and 47% on the whites. After final year-end expenses of $14,558, I realized a loss of 18% for 1972. This reflected the ups and downs of farming I had been told about, and I thought I had better get used to it if I were to continue. Fortunately, I had my Ecodyne salary, and when I averaged the two years of 1971 and 1972 for all our income, we would show a profit of 17%. . . . Not bad by Wall Street standards.

I was still bullish on being a part-time grower.

CHAPTER 4

Deeper Involvement

THE YEAR 1972 HAD BEEN BAD, not only for me, but for other growers as well. As a result, agricultural properties were beginning to appear for sale on the real estate market. I decided to begin looking for an additional property.

West Dry Creek Ranch

In early November, while scanning the classified ads in the Santa Rosa *Press Democrat* under Farms & Acreage, I saw an ad for 20 acres consisting of prunes and older vineyards for sale in Dry Creek valley for $65,000. It looked interesting so I contacted Catalani, the realtor, and asked if he knew about the property. He said the property was on upper West Dry Creek Road. It belonged to the Guadagni family, and eight family members had an equal one-eighth ownership share.

I immediately went to see the property. It had 7.5 acres on a steep slope that extended in a western direction upwards above the road, terminating at a forest evergreen border of fir and pine trees. High on the top were two acres of old head-pruned vines of Zinfandel and Carignane planted on 7' × 7' spacing. The steepness of the slope indicated that no cross cultivation was done, because tractor roll-over was a serious risk. Furthermore, cultivation by a crawler tractor that could work within the 84" row spacing had to be performed down slope only, rather than up slope, because small narrow tractors didn't have the horsepower to pull a cutting disk up such a steep incline. Moreover, even though row spacing was 84", the working width of a tractor had to be 50" or less for clearance of a head-pruned vine where the vine arms could extend 12" to 15" beyond the head of the vine.[7]

---

7 For example, if a large head-pruned vine had a maximum width of 30" across, that would allow only 2" side clearance with a 50"-gauge tractor. That's very tight.

At the bottom of the hill were a few mixed fruit trees, a large barn, a single detached garage, sheds, and a house. The house was a simple, old, single story ranch house built around 1920, with a screened back porch and a covered front porch. The house was in disrepair, and the oldest son of the family was currently living there alone. On the east side of the road, gently sloping towards Dry Creek, were 12.5 acres that contained seven acres of prunes, four acres of older mixed red vines, and a new one-acre block of one-year-old Zinfandel not yet in production. In the middle of this lower block was a shallow well where a small gas-powered pump would pump water at a low flow rate a distance of 1,000' across the road to a small redwood tank elevated 15' above the house. This tank would supply water to the house by gravity.

In spite of the state of disrepair, I liked what I saw. The place was a beautiful setting, and I could see potential in the property by removing prunes and planting premium grape varietals. Because of my bad experience in dealing directly with Simoni, I didn't want to deal directly with the owners of the Guadagni property, so I asked Catalani to intervene and make an offer on my behalf.

With eight different owners I was sure it would be a miracle if all eight could reach any agreement. To my astonishment, within a week, Catalani was able to secure acceptance from all eight shareowners of my offer of $65,000. Terms of the purchase contract included $15,000 down payment with the balance of $50,000 to be paid in full within two years. The owners would not carry a note on the balance, so I needed to secure financing. Remembering how Simoni reacted after he had agreed to sell, I had to move quickly before anyone changed their mind. I immediately contacted Equitable, and without delay, they agreed to consolidate my loan on the Simoni Ranch with the funding needed to buy the property, and to pay the Guadagni shareholders in full. The terms of the consolidated loan with Equitable were $88,000 principal to be paid in 24 annual payments of $3,500 at an interest rate of 8.5%, with a balloon payment of $7,500 due on January 1, 1975. The loan was approved on December 27, 1972, and I became the owner of the Guadagni property.

It was fortunate that I had established a prior relationship with Equitable so I could secure quick financing with a minimum of hassle and paperwork. I now had 44 acres to operate and was becoming more involved. I was still determined I could handle both responsibilities of my work with Ecodyne combined with being a part-time grape grower.

A Man Named Jim

I knew going forward that 1973 was going to be a new challenge for me. I realized 44 acres and two separated vineyards plus my ever-increasing Ecodyne responsibilities were going to test my physical endurance and ability to manage this total endeavor. I needed to find and develop some assistance from another person, and I needed to explore this immediately. That person was Jim Guadagni.

Jim Guadagni, 1973.

Jim was the sole relative living in the house on the West Dry Creek property. I soon began to establish a relationship with him that would be not only memorable, but invaluable. He was short and stocky, about 5'4" with sloping shoulders, a round bald head with deep-set eyes. Jim was 68 years old, born nearby in Cloverdale, California, to parents who had immigrated from Tuscany, Italy. He had three brothers and four sisters. Jim's father had purchased property in the upper Dry Creek Valley on Peña Creek where he had a small orchard and vineyard. He later purchased the 20-acre parcel that I would eventually end up buying. Jim's uniform of the day was always the same: faded blue bib overalls, long-sleeved blue or khaki shirt, and a crumbled-brim hat that shaded his weathered face. He had a pleasant calmness about him combined with a subtle chuckle when things amused him, and when he smiled it was evident that he was missing a few front teeth. He drove an older '65 Chevy pickup truck, but he never traveled very far from his ranch.

Jim went to school at the Peña Creek school house, but never went past the fourth grade. He dropped out to help his father work on the ranches. His education may have been cut short to help his father, yet I found him to be extremely intelligent and not misled by things that did not make sense to him. I knew he could write his name, but I'm sure his writing and reading abilities were limited. Jim had married in his early 20s and had two daughters. His wife left him without reason when the oldest daughter was only five years old, leaving him alone to raise the girls. Jim didn't drink or make wine. Yet he was proud to show me wine aging in barrels made by his brother. He told me that as a youngster, he had helped his father make wine, but I surmised he must have had a problem with alcohol and needed to withdraw from it entirely.

Jim was currently leasing a nearby 25-acre vineyard in addition to farming the 20-acre family ranch I had recently purchased. He asked if he could continue to live in the house and do some work for me to supplement his income from the leased vineyard. I was delighted he wanted to stay in the house and work for me, because it solved my problem of having to find someone to live in this rundown house, which might include some considerable fix-up expense. Jim had a TD 6 crawler tractor with all the equipment necessary to cultivate the vineyard, which meant I didn't need to transport my equipment 15 miles between the two vineyards. We made an agreement which allowed him to continue to live in the house for a rent of $70/month and act as caretaker of the property. He would be paid $2.50/hour for any vineyard work he performed on the property including reimbursement for any use of his farm equipment. Any additional field labor needed would be paid directly by me. It was a verbal agreement sealed by handshake . . . no rental agreement or written contract for vineyard work.

Jim did the majority of the vineyard work at Dry Creek throughout the growing season, which was fortunate since my responsibilities at Ecodyne, operating the 24 acres on the home ranch, and my family kept me busy. On weekends, I visited Jim and worked with him when time permitted. I learned a lot from him about being a wine grape grower. He had a wealth of information, and was eager to advise and offer the wisdom and experience he had acquired on growing grapes. He was an expert tractor driver and took great pride in how close he could cultivate to a vine without causing any damage. Not only did he teach me his methods regarding pruning, cultivation, and vine management, but he also introduced me to the practices of overhead irrigation, which would soon be added to my agenda.

In May, I purchased piping for my first overhead irrigation system to irrigate the lower 12 acres adjacent to Dry Creek. The system included 1,530' of 4" and 850' of 3" used, aluminum, portable pipe, plus 20 Rainbird impulse sprinklers. Pipe sections measured 20' in length and were connected with bell-and-spigot, quick-break, gasketed fittings. Sprinklers were attached to the pipe by 4'-high, ½"-diameter pipe risers, which could be shut off for servicing by closing a valve mounted on each riser inlet. The piping was completely portable. Piping was placed through the vineyard on 40' spacing, the sprinklers were spaced at 40', and the risers were held vertically by tying them to adjacent vine heads with twine. PG&E extended a power line from West Dry Creek Rd. to a pole and breaker panel near the creek. A nearby neighbor dug a sump hole with his backhoe in Dry Creek where a temporary suction line could be placed. The pump assembly consisted of a three-phase, 7½ hp, electric centrifugal pump that was mounted on a skid platform. The pump was dragged by tractor down to the creek, the suction line was connected, and the pump was plugged into the breaker panel. The irrigation cycle was controlled manually. I would start the system after setting the sprinklers; Jim would turn it off. The sprinklers emitted around 3.5 gpm at 30 psi. We would irrigate anywhere from 4-6 hours. This irrigation system provided the equivalent of ¾" to 1¼" of rain. When the irrigation cycle was complete, the system could be quickly broken down and moved over another 40'. Sloshing through the mud with rubber boots, it took two people two hours to move a 20′ section of pipe with sprinkler head attached. Jim and I did this work, but on occasion Anita would help.[8]

Jim took great pride in his work and the quality of the grapes produced on the ranch. We had an excellent relationship and I respected him for his knowledge and recognition by his peers in the surrounding area of upper Dry Creek Valley as a knowledgeable grape grower. I appreciated the way he treated me. My experience with Simoni had been quite the opposite.

Jim Forchini, Jim Guadagni (center), and Carla at West Dry Creek Ranch, 1975.

With Jim working and managing the 20-acre Dry Creek vineyard, and me doing the same on our 24-acre Old Redwood Highway home ranch, both vineyards had been pruned and fertilized by March 20, and we began cultivation on April 7. In May I planted 700 Zinfandel plants and 800 root stocks intended to be budded over to Pinot Noir on the home ranch that fall. By June 1st all suckering and dusting of both ranches had been done, and now it was time to relax a little and wait for harvest.

In early September the prunes were harvested by Jim, and I gave him the entire crop. He had taken care of them at his expense, and I had no interest in prunes and didn't want to get involved. What little value they had I was willing to forfeit as a measure of appreciation for his services to me this first year at Dry Creek.

We began the 1973 harvest at Dry Creek on September 15 with Jim in control. He would call and keep me posted on the progress, tonnage, and sugar measurements. On September

---

8 The practice of pumping directly from Dry Creek is no longer allowed as water usage soon became strictly regulated.

17 I used a week of vacation time to begin harvest at the home ranch. By September 20 we had completed the first round of harvest, and had picked 40 tons between the two vineyards. This was going to mean at least $22,000 in the bank, and I was elated and looked forward to what might be a very good and prosperous year.

On September 21, we enjoyed a brief break in the harvest as we waited for sugars to accumulate higher before resuming. This was a lucky break for me because I had previously committed to participate in a seminar on cooling towers in Los Angeles on September 26. Jumping on an early morning flight that day, I presented a paper at the School of Engineering, California State University, Los Angeles, on mechanical design and materials used in cooling tower equipment. Upon returning home that night, I began to realize there would be times when conflicts would arise between my job and the vineyards. Fortunately, this time it worked out . . . , but what about the future?

On September 29, I took my second week of paid vacation from Ecodyne and resumed harvest. By October 2 we had completed the first-crop harvest on both vineyards, and on October 19 we picked and sold 3.4 tons of second-crop Zinfandel to Korbel. The total crop produced was 72.5 tons: 56.9 tons from the home ranch and 15.6 tons from Dry Creek. The total was up 200% from 1972. The base price paid for Zinfandel was $500/ton at 21.0 Brix with a 7% bonus per point up to a maximum of 23.0 Brix. We averaged $570/ton with the bonus for Zinfandel, and the average price/ton, including white grapes and second-crop Zinfandel, came to $494/ton. This amounted to a gross payment of $33,389 . . . a nice supplement to my regular salary. In reality, the payment exceeded my salary. I could see the benefits of raising wine grapes on the side, as Bruce had suggested. After the harvest of 1973, I removed four acres of prunes at Dry Creek, burned the trees and fumigated the site in preparation for planting the following year with Cabernet Sauvignon.

To date, between 1971 and 1973, I had successfully managed my job responsibilities at Ecodyne and the operation of two vineyards. Provided I had Jim's help, it looked like I could handle this dual role of engineer and winegrower. If something happened to Jim, I would have to deal with it then. At this point, I was not going to worry about it.

Double-Duty Overtime

I started 1974 with full enthusiasm and vigor. My work at Ecodyne was going well, the family had settled into living in the country, and over the past three years, I had been able to manage both responsibilities as a full-time engineer and a part-time winegrower.

By the end of February, pruning on both vineyards was completed, and cultivation began in April. Later that month I planted four acres of Cabernet at Dry Creek. My confidence was building, and I was anticipating a new vintage season utilizing all that had been learned the past three years from Simoni and Guadagni, and learning by doing.

In the corporate world, 1974 would bring forth some important changes at Ecodyne that would present new challenges for me. With completion and wrap-up of all the new products that Don, Sam, and I had designed, these products were now in manufacturing and were being installed in new cooling towers all over the country. Sam had been previously transferred to the Erection Department, and now my boss, Don, chose to leave the company and his position as Vice President of Engineering, to do independent research and prototype development. With these management changes, the doors were closed on the New Product Development department.

Don, Sam, and I had been awarded a patent for a range of 60-300 hp herringbone, single-reduction gearboxes to power the fan that employed a unique, direct-drive, vertical mount, totally enclosed motor in the air stream. This eliminated the double-reduction gearbox previously used with an extended drive line and motor mounted on the deck outside the fan stack. Another patent had been awarded for a range of fiberglass, steel-reinforced fan blades in sizes from 12' to 30' diameter. The larger fan blades would pull over a million cubic feet of air per hour over the internal fill sections of the tower. After I took over as manager of NPD in 1970, seven more patents had been awarded for fiberglass flow valves, injection molded nozzles, a fiberglass distribution box, flexible pipe seals, and PVC louvers. Unlike the automobile industry, where new designs for body and internal parts are redesigned on a regular basis,

Jim Forchini promotion to Ecodyne Manager of Service Operations, 1974.

the new products we had designed were going to be around for a long time. . . . At least we hoped so.

Ecodyne had no plan to develop any additional new products at the time NPD ceased operations. There would be a manager of engineering at Ecodyne whose function would be to prepare structural drawings for field erection of both wood and concrete counterflow and crossflow towers. These various towers employed the new products that had been developed in the NPD department.

My salary as New Product Development Manager had increased 30% during the four-year period under my supervision. On March 11, 1974, Ecodyne made an organizational change, and I was assigned as Service Operations Manager reporting to the Vice President of Marketing at a salary increase of 9%. I was grateful for this additional salary increase, but I knew it would come with more company responsibilities. I was responsible for Customer

Service and product testing of cooling tower thermal performance, and I handled any problems with the new products that had been designed by the NPD department. The former Manager of Customer Service, and all personnel carrying out field assignments for new product installation or warranty service, reported to me. I had to travel more frequently to jobsites and was given an air travel card to book last minute flights. Cell phones were not in existence in those days, so I was given a phone card I could use to make calls without having to call collect or plunk in an amount of change. Airline travel was by economy, but I was not limited to a per diem amount for food and lodging provided such costs were within reason. Ecodyne did all they could to make my travel as comfortable and stress-free as possible, which I appreciated.

Mike Forchini (age 9) driving tractor, Old Redwood Highway Ranch, 1975.

On April 25, 1974, our third child, Andrew, was born, and my recent salary increases couldn't have come at a better time. The large house on the Old Redwood Highway home ranch property provided more than enough room for our increasing family, and the outdoor environment proved to be a great place for the kids to romp, take tractor rides, get dirty, and engage with nature. I was becoming more involved with major responsibilities at Ecodyne, and I knew my new Ecodyne position combined with the operation of two vineyards and a growing family of five was going to require double-duty overtime, stamina, and endurance.

In May, I had a 260' well drilled at the home ranch, and I installed a 20 hp submersible pump in an 8" casing. The well tested over 300 gpm at 40 psi and the water table draw down was only 23' from a starting depth of 29'. This was an excellent well whose location had been determined by a neighbor using a willow wand in a process known as *witching*. He was the go-to guy when it came to locating well sites. His credentials certainly were proven with my well when he claimed my well site was above the intersection of two underground aquifers. This single well would allow me to boost production, irrigate my older vineyards, and give the new and future plantings a quick boost into production. I installed an underground network of piping with vertical risers at locations where I could connect portable pipe with impulse sprinklers for irrigating the older vines. On the new vineyards I installed drip irrigation.

In September, I had the remaining 3½ acres of prunes removed from Dry Creek. I started to prepare myself for the 1974 harvest, which was expected to be even larger than the record harvest in 1973. I thought it might be a good idea to get established with more than one winery as insurance against any problems which might develop with a sole-source purchaser. This later proved to be a very good decision. Jim introduced me to Frei Brothers in Dry Creek valley, a cooperative partially owned by the Gallo Brothers. I was also able to establish a commitment from Chateau Souverain, owned at the time by Lee Stewart, who had recently moved his winery from Napa Valley to Sonoma County's Alexander Valley. I continued to sell Zinfandel to Seghesio on a co-op basis, and I established a buyer for all our white grapes with Sotoyome Winery, a small winery located up the hill on Limerick Lane close to our home ranch.

Harvest began two weeks later this year. Jim started on October 1 at Dry Creek, and I took my two-week vacation and started harvest on October 2 at the home ranch. By October 15 we had finished harvesting both vineyards, picking 18 tons from Dry Creek and 74 tons at the home vineyard. This 92-ton crop was 27% above last year, and I was expecting a nice little secondary paycheck which would come in handy now that we were a family of five. However, the average price paid by Souverain and Frei Bros for Zinfandel turned out to be only $304/ton, down over 35% from 1973 prices. At Seghesio, it turned out to be even worse, and a complete disaster for the growers who had delivered there. Seghesio crushed over 3,000 tons of Zinfandel that yielded 562,000 gallons of wine. However, 1974 would be a fateful year for marketing, and the Seghesios were unable to secure a good price for the wine. With their backs to the wall, they were forced to take 50 cents a gallon whereas the market price was about $1.50/gal. After deducting processing costs of $40/ton, the net payment to each grower was only $47/ton. This low price was more than $250/ton less than average prices paid that year by Frei Brothers and Souverain, and it was down $520/ton from what Seghesio had paid me in 1973. Even though our 1974 tonnage was up sharply from 1973, the gross income was down 35% due to lower prices for Zinfandel and particularly the heavy loss from the grapes sold to Seghesio.

Later that year, Seghesio winery sent a letter to all their growers explaining the sad circumstances, backed up by an accounting with numbers, that led to the $47/ton payment. At that time Seghesio had only one buyer for the large quantity of bulk wine they had to sell, and they were forced to either take the offer of 50 cents a gallon or forget it. They had no other options but to take what was offered, knowing it was going to be a hardship for many of their loyal growers who had faithfully delivered to them over the years. Seghesio asked their growers not to be too bitter and remember the good times of the past. But many growers were very upset. As for me, I harbored no grudge because I had averaged $242/ton that year between the four different wineries. Moreover, my Ecodyne salary was still there. I appreciated that Seghesio had accepted my grapes when I first started as a newcomer in 1971, and I was thankful that delivering grapes to Seghesio eliminated a long-distance drive to Asti. Seghesio had paid me well from 1971 to 1973, they were a good family with a long history in the wine business, and I liked the members of the family whom I had met and dealt with. After 1974, Seghesio stopped crushing grapes from growers on a co-op basis and processed fruit only from their own vineyards.

In addition to the unfortunate monetary loss incurred from the deliveries to Seghesio, I had an equally bad contractual experience with Souverain during this harvest. After delivering over 29 tons to Souverain, it seems they did not like me contesting their sugar test readings. The tester on the sugar stand determined a sugar reading of 21.5 Brix when I made the last 5-ton gondola delivery of Petite Sirah. My testing in the vineyard before delivery recorded an average 23.0 Brix, so I thought their sugar stand reading was low. When I asked the tester how he calibrated his refractometer, he told me it was done by the winery in their lab using winery standard sugar solutions. This sounded strange to me since most refractometers are calibrated against distilled water, which is sugarless. More important, the sugar tester is supposedly a third party, unrelated to the winery. Upon hearing what the sugar tester said, I reached for my handy refractometer, which I carried in the glove box of my truck. In the same sugar stand solution that produced a reading of 21.5 Brix I measured 22.5 Brix. The disparity between my field 23.0 Brix measurement and the 22.5 Brix measurement from the gondola sample was reasonable, since the gondola sample would include more berries. What I didn't like was the disparity of 1.0 Brix in readings between the sugar stand tester and my reading on the same sample. Furthermore, in my mind it was unethical for the winery to calibrate their refractometer themselves, instead of using calibration by an independent third party, because sugar measurement affects the price paid per ton. In this case, there was a small sugar bonus paid on grapes delivered above 22.0 Brix. I proceeded to go into the winery to discuss my grievance but was quickly dismissed. After I had returned home, Souverain called to say "**don't come back**," insinuating I was a troublemaker. I still had unpicked Petite Sirah to harvest and was able to sell the grapes to Seghesio. The delivered grapes measured 23.5 Brix on the sugar stand.

By this point in my career as a winegrower, I was starting to see the ups and downs of agriculture. You had to expect price fluctuation based on supply, demand, and weather. Of equal importance, you had to deal with different wineries and submit to their requirements and policies of operation. All the grapes I sold in 1974 were without any written contracts because the wineries would not commit to specific prices. This was the norm. Wineries would accept your grapes, and you trusted they would be fair and give you a good price. Certainly, there were some small wineries with established brands that contracted small lots from designated growers at a specific price. However, for the large majority of winegrowers during this time period, you only had a vague idea of the base price to be paid, there was no guarantee, and you operated on the basis of faith and trust. Only when the check came in the mail did you know the price/ton, and at that point you were either happy or disappointed. In most any other business, this would be a very bad way to operate, but for winegrowers this is the way it was done.

I had barely completed the 1974 harvest, and was looking forward to a slower pace of activity when unexpectedly, out of the blue, I was advised on October 22 that my current boss, the Vice President of Marketing, was being promoted to Executive Vice President. It was further announced that as Manager of Service Operations, I would be part of a management group reporting directly to the President along with the new Executive Vice President, an internal appointment for a new Vice President of Marketing, the Vice President of Finance, and the Manager of Administration. My job title remained the same, but I was given another 8% salary increase on top of the 19% increase I had received seven months earlier. I thought this might mean more responsibility and travel would be forthcoming. I was now in the class of some heavy Company management, and I pondered what lay ahead. My development within the Company was moving very fast, my head was spinning, and I began to wonder where this corporate world of chair shuffling organization charts was headed. I wondered what would be expected from me going forward. Would the stress that I was working under become a problem? What might be the impact on my family life, my health, and my part-time involvement as a winegrower?

CHAPTER 5

Full-Time Winegrower

I BEGAN 1975 WITH THE DETERMINATION TO SUCCEED in this dual role of Service Operations Manager and winegrower. I was optimistic I could do it because I was 37 years old and in good health, had the support of my family, and had a tremendous asset in Jim Guadagni working with me in support of the two vineyards. I was very happy and fortunate to be part of the management group reporting to the Ecodyne president. I considered this a prestigious upper management position with opportunity for advancement and increased salary. Ecodyne had treated me well with salary increases and were very cordial towards my wife and children. The Company provided many social perks and engagements to keep employees happy and content. If Ecodyne was concerned about my involvement as a part-time winegrower, they certainly didn't show it. They were aware of this activity, seemed to accept it, and on many occasions would ask how things were going in the vineyards. Others in the Company were involved in winegrowing on the side, but they were not at the same management level as me. That is, they did not report to the company president.

Major Transition

In May of that year, and only seven months after I had been assigned to report to the president of Ecodyne, he resigned to a full and final retirement. And another important organization change was announced. The Executive Vice President, my current boss, was now promoted to be the new president of Ecodyne, and I would continue to report to him. On May 22, 1975, I received a personal hand-written note from the former president about how pleased he had been with my work and complimenting me on doing a good job of handling the many challenges of being the Service Operations Manager. He went on to say everyone in the top management group was enthusiastic about my performance and encouraged me to keep up the fine work. It made me feel good that he had such complimentary things to say about me. I liked the former president. He was very personable and pleasant, took great interest in my wife and family, was a great sports fan like me, and had taken me to sports banquets, which I enjoyed. I was going to miss him.

Soon thereafter, on June 12, 1975, the new Ecodyne president, who was still my current boss, made an important formal announcement to all employees. Posting on various Company bulletin boards, he announced the hiring of a new Vice President of Engineering to fill the vacant spot left by Don in 1974. I was surprised by this announcement, especially when I learned who this new person was. The person hired was John, a former employee who had previously worked in the Thermal Department while I was working in New Product Development. John was a member of the management group reporting to the president, yet I had not been apprised beforehand of this change. John and I were hired at about the same time in 1967 when the Company operated as Fluor Cooling Products. We were the same age, had been friends, and our wives were also socially connected. We were both young, energetic engineers and worked hard within our respective departments.

At the time, no one in engineering was using computer technology for design purposes; designs were done by hand, using calculators. Ecodyne's IBM computer was used mainly for administration, payroll, and inventory. John had knowledge of computer programming using FORTRAN, and prior to leaving Ecodyne in 1974, he had developed a thermal rating program which could analyze various options on fill packing configurations using our newly developed PVC fill packing.[9] While John was at Ecodyne, I learned the basics of FORTRAN programming from him, and I developed a program for fan blade design using lift and drag coefficients of aeronautical blade sections at various angles of attack and air flow velocities to determine lift. The final design would result in a tapered blade width with an objective of uniform air flow over the entire blade length. The program would calculate cubic feet per minute air flow against resistance of the tower's fill packing, from which the required fan motor horsepower could be determined. This fan design program proved to be fairly accurate after testing fans on a full-scale concrete crossflow tower cell built at Ecodyne to test fill packing and the fans.

After three years the relationship between John and me had gone from being socially close to company cordial. At about the same time, I had been promoted to Manager of New Product Development, and John had resigned from Ecodyne to go back east. He secured a management position in industrial cooling with a large equipment manufacturing company.

---

9   FORTRAN (FORmula TRANslation) was a computer program that could be used to perform complex calculations, usually for an engineering application. Some people called FORTRAN a computer language. It wasn't really a language, but a large collection of commands that could be put together to carry out calculations according to an algorithm modeled by the computer programmer. FORTRAN was popular in the engineering professions during the 1960s and 1970s.

I never heard about his progress or success after he left. Now, after a brief absence he was returning to Ecodyne reporting to the new president and was given a new title of Vice President of Engineering-Operations. I was disappointed to learn this because my boss, who was now the new president, had discussed informally with me that I might be under consideration for Vice President of Engineering. Maybe this was a form of dangling a carrot to get my response. I was pleased and showed gratitude for this consideration, however silently questioned whether I would really want this position. Was it feasible to think I could assume additional company responsibility of being Vice President of Engineering, maintain my involvement as a winegrower managing 44 acres of vineyards, and be a father to three young children, a husband, and head of household? However, there was no need for me to worry about being Vice President of Engineering now that John had been selected and the appointment had been announced. Maybe I hadn't shown enough enthusiasm for the job when the possibility had been discussed previously. Regardless of how I felt, I would still be part of the management group reporting to the president along with the other vice presidents. But I could foresee possible conflict working with my former peer and now the new VP of Engineering-Operations. When I considered that he would be overseeing engineering operations, that probably meant I could be reporting to him at some later time. On reflection, I questioned the motive of the former president's encouraging letter to me of May 22 and why the new president had initiated another 8% salary increase for me on June 23, 19 days before the announcement of the new VP of Engineering-Operations. The kind letter and salary raise were nice, but they were obviously intended to sway me to accept new organizational changes that might be forthcoming, and to deter me from possibly resigning. Ecodyne had a history of making frequent organizational changes, and the possibility of having to report to my former peer did not suit me well.

I was at a crossroad. Anita and I needed to discuss this matter quickly. Should I stay with the Company and maintain my dual role as Service Operations Manager and part-time winegrower? Should I not worry about any potential organizational changes that might never happen, or whether changes might not be in my best interests? Would it be better to resign from the corporate world and dedicate myself to a career as a winegrower? If I did resign, I knew I would lose a regular salary, and would give up three days paid holidays, company-paid vacations, and company-paid health insurance benefits. Could we make it on an income solely from grape growing?

The Company salary and extra winegrower income was great, but Company responsibilities had increased tremendously, and being a winegrower operating 44 acres of vineyards in two different locations was leading me towards a serious addiction: becoming a workaholic. To do justice to both employments meant all work, little play, lots of family sacrifice, and the possibility that over-commitment could have harmful effects on my health.

On the brighter side, the wine industry in Sonoma County was moving forward and the future looked promising. I enjoyed growing wine grapes, and I liked the many fine people I had met as a winegrower and the social attractions of industry events. As a winegrower you were self-employed. You were the boss. I found the healthy outdoor lifestyle working in the vineyards to be both physically and mentally therapeutic. Upon resigning from Ecodyne, I would be able to spend more time with my family on my schedule, not on my employer's schedule. I did not like being unable, or stretched such, that I could not find time to do things after work that young fathers do with growing children—like coaching little league, getting involved with school activities, and 4H involvement.

It was time for us to make up our minds. After a day of careful thought, Anita and I decided it would be best to resign from Ecodyne and commit to a change toward a new lifestyle. We decided to make a career change after 15 years that included three years in aerospace with JPL, four years in production engineering with OCLI, and eight years in new product development and management with Ecodyne. During those last four years, I had combined my profession in engineering with becoming a winegrower. Now we would dedicate ourselves to becoming full-time winegrowers with the objectives of upgrading our vineyards and possibly, building a small estate winery.

Engineering had been very good to me. It taught me skills in mechanical design, problem solving, innovative thinking, learning by doing, personnel management, technical writing, contracts, procurement, working with vendors, sales engineering, and customer service. All these skills would be valuable assets and important tools in my toolbox that I would bring forward and use as a winegrower. I would still have my mechanical engineering degree, and I planned to study for my professional engineering license. If necessary, I could do engineering consulting on the side, or return to engineering if winegrowing did not work out. Of utmost importance, I had Anita's complete support and encouragement. And I knew the kids would be happy that I would be staying put and not travelling on business. With resolve, optimism, and determination, we made the decision to face the future as full-time winegrowers. This was a major transition for the family.

The day after I had heard that a new Vice President of Engineering-Operations was coming on board, I did not go to work. Instead, I made a phone call from home to the Manager of Administration to tell him that I was resigning and that a formal letter of my resignation would be forthcoming. I soon received a personal handwritten letter from the new president expressing his sorrow and asking me to reconsider. He wanted me to wait until July 7, when he and the new Vice President of Engineering-Operations could sit down and talk with me about going forward and my alternatives. I never responded to his letter. As far as I was concerned, it was over. I had made up my mind. On June 16, 1975, four days after I had read the notice that John, the new Vice President of Engineering-Operations, was being hired, I sent my formal letter of resignation to Ecodyne, which expressed my gratitude for the opportunities, experience and promotions given me over a dynamic and exciting period of eight years. I wished the Company well.[10]

Had it not been for my employment with Fluor/Ecodyne, I would never would have met Bruce and, probably, I would never have become a winegrower.

Sink or Swim

On June 17, 1975, I became a full-time winegrower at the age of 37. I took no break after my resignation from Ecodyne. Instead, I launched quickly into my second career with determination to succeed. On that first day as a winegrower, as I drove my Ford Courier pickup down the driveway from the home vineyard, an unusual feeling came over me. For the first time in my life, I felt a strange state of mind and an unfamiliar sense of who I was and where I was going. When I approached the Old Redwood Highway, I normally would be turning left heading for Ecodyne, but instead I was turning right heading for my Dry Creek vineyard. I wasn't dressed in my usual sport coat, tie, and slacks. Now it was jeans, a denim work shirt, and sturdy work shoes. When I got to Dry Creek, Jim might be there, but he was usually off at the crack of dawn to work his leased vineyard or have breakfast with his daughter, who lived nearby. If he wasn't around, I would be all alone in the quiet solitude of my vineyard. There would be no one in an office to say "good morning." There would be no coffee break with other Ecodyne employees at the 9:45 AM food truck to talk business or engage in social conversation. My day would focus on two worn-out Sonoma County farms, spaced miles apart, with a lot of physical work waiting to be done. Was this really going to be me going forward? Yes, it was. This was real; this was what I decided upon and now, it was either . . . ***sink or swim!***

Jim Guadagni would continue to live on the Dry Creek property and was there to help if I needed a hand, but now I was the full-time winegrower and I took over the operation of the Dry Creek vineyard. My vineyards had got off to a good start for the new vintage year, and by February 1, with Jim's help, we had all pruning completed at Dry Creek and at the home ranch. Now that the prunes had been completely removed, I could devote all operations to wine grapes, and on April 7, Jim and I began to disk under the cover crops at both ranches. Things were going well, until on the night of April 16, we had frost, and temperatures dropped to 29°F, burning all the white grapes with 2-3" *shoots*, and some young Zinfandels with 1" shoots. A cold spring prevailed, and second growth on the frosted

---

10 Ecodyne Cooling Towers is no longer in operation at the former site in Windsor, CA. It is now a division of Ecodyne Limited headquartered in Burlington, Ontario, Canada. The original full scale concrete test cell where fans and fill packing tests were conducted is still standing and can be seen by looking south approximately 200 yards from Lot 3 of the Contractor Storage yard at 930 Shiloh Rd. in Windsor, CA.

vines was slow and irregular. This frost would contribute to a large loss in production for the year. It wasn't going to be easy.

I had to move equipment and materials back and forth between the two vineyards. The one-way distance was 12 miles and took almost an hour driving slowly with my 20-year-old 1½ ton flatbed Ford truck. My route led me north on the two-lane Old Redwood Highway, across the Russian River, bypassing the town of Healdsburg using circumventing roads, then seven miles north on narrow Dry Creek Rd., across Dry Creek, north on West Dry Creek Road for two miles on a narrow curving road, across Peña Creek, and finally arriving at my vineyard. Adding to this time, was the loading and unloading of the tractor on the back of the truck and chaining it down. Each procedure took about half an hour. To make things easier, I made a loading ramp by cutting into a side hill. With heavy planks, the ramp enabled me to drive the tractor directly on and off the truck. I hated moving heavy equipment, and I thought how great it would be to have duplicate equipment at each vineyard. But at this time, such luxury was unaffordable.

The growing season passed quickly, with my vineyard management work on both vineyards. This included cultivation, suckering, sulfur dusting, and irrigation. I tried to do as much as possible by myself, but I did hire workers for suckering and hoeing around the vine base. I could move the portable aluminum pipe sections by myself, but on occasion Jim or Anita would help me. All the while Anita and the kids were happy to have me around, home for lunch, and not displaced to some far-off location working on cooling tower issues.

In early September, I made cuttings in my vineyard from healthy old vine Zinfandel, and, using a *notch-graft* technique known as *budding*, I inserted buds on *St. George rootstock* planted where vines had been missing. The bud had to match the notch perfectly and was secured in place by a rubber band wrapped tight around the rootstock. After wrapping the bud, the vine was completely covered with a mound of dirt for protection through the winter. In the following spring the rootstock would be uncovered, the band cut, and the bud would be gently pushed to test for a successful *graft*. If the graft was successful, a milk carton would be placed around the rootstock to protect the emerging bud. I learned this budding technique by watching experienced grafters, and I had moderate success when only a few vines were involved. But when many vines needed budding, I would hire an experienced grafting crew.

Harvest began on September 26, with the first picking of two tons of new Pinot Noir that had been planted in 1972. The Pinot paid $385/ton. Thereafter, the pace proceeded rapidly and harvest at Dry Creek started on September 29. I had recruited my own crew from workers who had picked for me in the past, or drop-in laborers looking for work. The weather in mid-October turned bad, and we had four inches of rain, which drenched the vineyard floor resulting in mud, some rot, and a drop in sugar that delayed the harvest for a short while. By October 20 the harvest from both vineyards had been completed. The crop from Dry Creek was only 6.6 tons and the overall combined tonnage from both vineyards was 51.1 tons, down 45% from 1974. The low tonnage was related to damage from the April frost, poor berry set, *shatter*, and harvest rain that made some grapes unsuitable because of rot. The income for 1975 was only $13,471, down 38%. The average price paid on black grapes was $295/ton and whites $136/ton.

Now that I was self-employed, the ups and downs of prices and production that I had experienced over the past five years started to concern me. Over the first two years, from 1971 to 1972, when operating only the home vineyard, I averaged 37.5 tons a year, producing an average income of $14,672 a year. Over the next three years, from 1973 to 1975, operating both the home and Dry Creek vineyards, I produced an average of 72 tons a year which paid an average gross yearly amount of $23,641. During this five-year period my vineyard income was in addition to my Ecodyne salary. My salary with Ecodyne had been stable and progressed upward over seven years at an average rate increase of 15% a year. But as a full-time winegrower, I had no salary income and was now subjected to unpredictable grape prices and production. I had some serious thinking to do about my future as a winegrower. I realized I was going to have to **sink or swim.**

Quick Action Required

I started 1976 on a cautious note. I knew that an average yearly income of $23,641 for a growing family of five might not be good enough. If we were to continue, we would have to change our lifestyle from when I was working two jobs as engineer and winegrower. We couldn't always count on a record crop like in 1974, or high prices like in 1973. We would need to have some evidence blended with a more realistic optimism in 1976, to convince us that we were on the right path. As an insurance measure, I began to study for my professional engineering license, thinking I might need it to do some independent engineering consulting to augment my vineyard income.

The year 1976 began extremely dry. There had been no appreciable rain past December 1975, and no rain in January of 1976. January temperatures had been warm (in the low 70s), and there was growing concern that an early bud push would be vulnerable to frost. In February, we received 2½ inches of rain, and less than an inch in March. It was very dry in the vineyards, and on the night of April 2, frost was predicted, and temperatures dropped to 30°F. Established growers had their wind machines and sprinklers working, and smudge pots burning to protect their crops. I had none of this, but I used a new product I had seen at a trade show that was made by Mobil Oil Co. It was an incendiary block in the shape of a 12" cube that you set out on a pattern on the vineyard floor and ignited. The blocks burned slowly, producing a 1 to 2 degree increase in temperature near ground level. I placed the blocks in my Pinot vineyard which had had an early bud break on March 28. The burning blocks worked well, and no damage was observed the next day.[11]

I continued with cultivation, dusting, and irrigation through the summer. In July it was evident that the Zinfandel crop would be off due to shatter and the inclusion of many shot berries. *Shot berries* were small pea-like green berries that never develop, resulting in bunches 50-70% of normal weight. However, the Pinot looked good, as did the Carignane and Petit Sirah.

I began Dry Creek harvest on September 13 and finished on September 27, picking a total of 12 tons, up 81% from 1975. I started picking Old Redwood Highway (ORH) on September 15, and finished on October 22, for a total of 58 tons, up 30% from 1975. The average price paid for Zinfandel was $360/ton, up 19% from 1975, but Pinot had dropped in price to $300/ton. My overall income was $20,371, up 51 % from 1975, but down 11% from my past-four-year average.

The year 1976 had the distinction of being the second driest year in recorded history since 1888. Between July 1, 1976, and June 30, 1977, only 16.8" of rain was received, which was about 4" below minimal requirements for a decent crop. Had it not been for some unseasonable rains in August and September of 1977, the 1977 harvest could have been much worse.

I had taken four crops from the Guadagni Dry Creek property between 1973-1976, averaging only 2.1 tons/acre, a production level considered well below sustainable. It wasn't hard to see that without my former salary, we would be living on a very tight budget and would have to make sacrifices. The home ranch (ORH) had decent production, but Dry Creek was below average, and the new Cabernet vineyard I had planted would not come into production for three more years. I was also becoming concerned about growing Cabernet on the fertile valley floor. This location for Cabernet was not in high demand and top prices would be hard to get. The vines would develop a vigorous canopy of entangled canes, the fruit would be shaded, and mildew would be hard to control. High sugar development would be difficult to achieve, and delayed ripening and harvest would make the grape vulnerable to rain that sometimes occurred in late October.

At this point I realized that if I were to remain a full-time winegrower, I had better look for another ranch that would yield a higher production of quality fruit. Hopefully a new property closer to the home ranch would make moving equipment easier.

---

11 Effective as they were, these slow-burning blocks and smudge pots are no longer approved for use since they contribute to air pollution.

A Man Named LeBrett

I didn't think I would have any problem selling my West Dry Creek vineyard because a close neighbor, Lou Preston, was looking for additional property in this upper Dry Creek area. I first met Lou Preston in 1973 after he had recently purchased the Hartsock property which bordered Peña Creek. Lou was a few years younger than me, and I got to know him better each time we met. He came from outside the industry, and I learned his objectives were the same as mine. He had an interest in grapes and was beginning a new career as a winegrower. He was also eager to start a small winery, which he eventually did in 1975 by making wine in a small old shed located on his property that had been used for dehydrating prunes.

After deciding I would start looking for a larger vineyard, I searched for vineyard or farm property in the local newspaper, just like I did in finding the Guadagni property. I didn't see any advertised listings for property that caught my attention. My thoughts eventually led me back to 1971, when Simoni and I had borrowed a fertilizer spreader from a grower who operated his vineyard on the elevated eastern bench land of Dry Creek. I remembered the owner was getting on in age, and that the property was somewhat run down. As I remembered, it had large plantings of older head-pruned vines with a few fruit trees scattered about. The acreage was of significant size, and the elevated setting above the valley floor was unique, with beautiful views west to the hills and east to the ridges bordering Dry Creek Valley.

I contacted Catalani, the realtor, and told him that I wanted to sell West Dry Creek and re-invest in property which had greater grape production and better future potential. I mentioned the ranch that I had visited five years earlier with Simoni, and I asked if he would be willing to inquire about who owned the property, and determine if it was for sale, or might the owner consider selling. After I showed him the location of the property, Catalani said he knew who the owner was, and he would make an inquiry on my behalf.

To my amazement, in the same manner in which he had quickly secured signatures on sales agreement of the Guadagni property, Catalani quickly came back to tell me that the owner was a man named Paul LeBrett, who was 67 years old and might be interested in selling under the right terms and conditions. Paul was living in Healdsburg in a comfortable newer home with his wife, who had recently had open heart surgery. LeBrett had a married son and daughter, but at this time neither of them was interested in continuing to operate the ranch.

Paul LeBrett was a first-generation Italian. Born in Ohio in 1910, after his mother and father had immigrated to America from the Calabria region of Italy. The name LeBrett didn't resonate with me as Italian. It sounded more French. But I never questioned his nationality, and I never asked Paul about his surname. Later I was told by some of Paul's relatives that

Paul's father had changed his name upon entry to Ellis Island. The name change apparently was motivated by fear of being tracked down in revenge over some bad incident that had occurred in Italy involving Paul's grandfather.

Paul was short, medium build, mild mannered, and pleasant in appearance. He spoke fluent Italian. As I got to know him, I found him to be a very decent, soft-spoken man with a never-ending warm smile and lighthearted personality. He would occasionally enjoy speaking short Italian phrases to me to see if I could pick up on what he was saying.

Paul's father was working for the railroad in Ohio when he started to develop health problems attributed to the harsh winter climate of Ohio. In 1916 he began to search for work in a warmer

Paul LeBrett

environment, and his search led to sunny California where the family settled in San Francisco for a brief period. He soon realized that San Francisco could be cold and damp in the summer due to fog and heavy marine layers coming onshore from the Pacific Ocean. After a brief stay in San Francisco, he was referred to Sonoma County and its warmer climate. He found employment working in agriculture within the vineyards and orchards of Dry Creek Valley. The work, the environment, and the pleasant weather in Sonoma County all being to his liking, he decided Dry Creek Valley would be the family home, and he sent for his wife (Paul's mother) to come join him.

The LeBretts' property was located on the main Dry Creek Road, which ran parallel and east of Dry Creek heading north towards Lake Sonoma. It was four miles closer to our Old Redwood Highway home ranch than the upper West Dry Creek Guadagni property. It consisted of two separate parcels totaling 67 acres. The LeBrett property had formerly been part of the larger Kelly ranch, which had an early history from the late 1800s of growing Mission grapes, fruit, and olives. Five Kelly children (two girls and three boys) had inherited the ranch, which was later subdivided and owned by seven different owners who would plant prunes and Zinfandel grapes. Two of the Kelly boys had no children, the other boy was killed in an accident: one of the Kelly girls also had no children, and the other sister had one girl. No Kellys were living in the area at the time, and no one seemed to know where any of them could be found.

Paul's father purchased 31 acres of the ranch in 1936. The acreage had been owned by a woman who had purchased the property from a German man, who had bought it in 1918 from one of the Kelly brothers. She had it for only four years. At the time of the LeBrett purchase, the property had been planted with 15 acres of Zinfandel. In the 1940s Paul and his father planted additional Zinfandel vines. In 1951 Paul and his mother purchased another 36 adjoining acres from the Kelly sister who had no children. The property had been planted to Carignane grapevines and prunes, and it contained some small quantities of mixed red and white grapes and some fig, apple, and persimmon fruit trees. Paul removed most of the prunes and planted more Zinfandel vines.

Paul's mother died in 1958, his father in 1961, and upon their passings, Paul inherited the entire ranch. Of the combined 67 acres, approximately 40 acres were older head-pruned, non-irrigated Zinfandel, Carignane, and Petite Sirah. Interplanted within the blocks were a smattering of white Chasselas and red Alicante, along with a few remaining prune and fruit trees. The balance of 27 acres was mostly an unplanted watershed covered with manzanita, madrone, and scrub oak rising above the bench land of the vineyards. This watershed contained two springs that fed a shallow pond behind an earthen dam close to the vineyards.

Paul told me the vineyard would produce an average total production of about 150 tons/year, which seemed likely to me, although I saw no receipts nor asked for any documents that would substantiate this claim. When dealing with these older Italian grape growers, you had to trust and show respect for what you were told, or you ran the risk of losing the sale. All the grapes were sold to Allied Grape Growers at Asti. Equipment that would be included in any sale included a Cat D2 crawler tractor, a mold board plow, a cultivator, a 1947 Chevy 1½ ton flatbed truck, a grape box conveyor, and some wooden grape boxes.

There was a 400'-long, unimproved, narrow gravel entrance road leading along a narrow draw to four separate buildings located along the right side of the entrance road. There was a small wooden storage barn for supplies and tools, a tractor and truck shed which leaned to the right, a Quonset hut cluttered with evidence of farm labor inhabitants from prior days, and an old house that was currently rented to some others. The old two-bedroom house, which had been built in 1924, had a bathroom and kitchen, and was simple in design without any distinctive features other than a nice brick fireplace. It really was more a cabin than a house. The exterior siding was shiplap redwood, and the main floor was supported by posts on cement blocks. The floors in each of the rooms sagged owing to this marginal foundation. A second story had been added in 1934, and in 1964 LeBrett had added family and laundry rooms. The second-floor addition was unfinished on the interior. The building framing was rough and exposed; there was no insulation, so porcelain knob-and-wire could be seen hanging from rafters. Numerous folding beds on the second story indicated they had been used as living quarters. I assumed they were for temporary vineyard workers. The family and laundry additions were of poor quality, evidently hastily constructed as low-budget add-ons. All four buildings showed neglect and needed serious repair. A 6' well by the barn contained a submersible pump that supplied water of good flow and quality to the house. House sewage and grey water were discharged to a buried redwood sump box from which effluent discharged by slow leakage underground. There was a large refuse area of discarded junk, truck frames, bottles, and cans dumped in a ravine at the back of the property. It was obvious this property would involve a lot of work for both vineyard and property clean up.

Catalani told me LeBrett was willing to carry a 10-year note on the property, so on October 14, 1976, I made an unsolicited offer of $190,000. The terms were a down payment of $55,000 and a promissory 10-year note to LeBrett, secured by a first deed of trust, in the amount of $135,000 bearing 8% interest. Annual payments of $6,500 on the principal plus interest would be paid in December, with a final balloon payment on the outstanding balance at the end of the 10-year term. The offer was contingent upon my ability to sell the West Dry Creek property within 90 days, and to secure Equitable approval for an early final payoff of $10,386 without penalty on my outstanding $88,000 loan. Based on my former bad experience with Simoni, I added an addendum to the sales agreement that included a listing of all equipment that went with the property. I also added the right to develop the property by removal of buildings as I found necessary, including removal and replanting of older vineyards, road development, and pond improvements. I agreed to remove no more than five acres at a time and would replant before removing additional vineyard acreage. I also gave Paul exclusive rights to enter the ranch to observe operations or go mushroom and deer hunting as he had done in the past. But no more refuse was to be dumped on the property.

Selling West Dry Creek was not a problem since my neighbor Preston was eager to buy. We quickly agreed on a selling price of $110,000 for West Dry Creek. Equitable agreed to a reconveyance on my note, and we entered escrow on November 22. After paying Equitable the $10,386 balance on my note plus closing costs, $99,000 was transferred to my bank savings. I paid $55,000 to LeBrett, signed a note with him for $135,000, and retained $44,000 in the bank to be used for ranch development.

On December 6, 1976 I became the owner of the LeBrett property at 5143 Dry Creek Road.

Growing Big With Caution

I began 1977 with optimistic enthusiasm. I now had both the LeBrett and Simoni properties, 91 acres to care for, of which about 60 acres were vineyards, mostly old but still very productive. This meant a larger crop than I had previously experienced might develop. I was depending on larger production and rising grape prices to provide a sustainable income going forward, which would cover both vineyard and family expenses.

But there was no guarantee of good weather, rising grape prices, or consistent, large, productive crops. I thought it might be wise to be cautious and have a contingency plan to earn additional income. I revisited my earlier thoughts of obtaining my professional engineering license. It had been only two years since I left engineering employment, but the technology, discipline, nuts-and-bolts were still fresh in my head, and I didn't want to let that mindset go stale. I thought it might be valuable to have such a license, so I made the commitment to study for the license while the time was right.

Over many hours of studying at night after operating the vineyards by day, I reviewed all the disciplines of mechanical engineering using the textbooks and papers I had from Cal Poly. I obtained samples of former test questions and took my six-hour examination in San Francisco in the winter of 1977. On March 9, 1977, I was informed I had passed the examination and was awarded Certificate No. 18035 as a duly registered Professional Engineer in Mechanical Engineering by the State of California Department of Consumer Affairs. This gave me some peace of mind.

Eager to give it a try, I soon branded myself as Applied Engineering Services, purchased stationery, and had a rubber stamp made bearing my certificate number, name, and title. I wrote proposals to several wineries offering my services in mechanical design, problem solving, and related technical services. After a few months of inactivity and no interest, I did secure some work reviewing fire sprinkler installations that needed approval by a professional engineer. It became apparent, however, that the need for my services was not what I had hoped, and that developing a market for my services would take a lot more time and pursuit. Whatever I was offering was either already being provided in-house, or by manufacturer representatives. I concluded my contingency plan would be best served by maintaining my registration in good standing, paying the annual renewal fees, and keeping my rubber stamp handy for future use, if needed. I decided not to invest any more time soliciting technical services, thinking it would be better to concentrate on my major objective of vineyard development.

In early June 1977, the cluster count looked very good on both ranches, and with a little luck it looked possible that I might harvest a big crop. However, Sonoma County was experiencing another year of drought, and by the end of June we had only received 14.9" of rain in Healdsburg, which was the lowest rainfall since records were kept. This record low rainfall followed the second lowest total of 16.8" recorded the previous year. The dry conditions resulted in shatter, a condition of poor pollination and berry set on the Pinot Noir, and loose stringy clusters with multiple green shot berries on the Zinfandel. My expectations for a big 1977 crop were beginning to fade. To further add to my concern, triple digit temperature (110°F) occurred on August 1, which resulted in berry dehydration that would reduce cluster weight and total production tonnage.

Then in mid-September a miracle happened. . . . Someone, somewhere said a prayer or did a rain dance. Mother Nature opened the heavens, and we received over 2" of rain between September 17 and 19; this was followed by another inch on September 26. The 3" of rain just before harvest gave the dehydrated grapes a good drink and pumped up their cluster weight. We picked as fast as we could to avoid rot, and by October 13 we had finished picking both ranches. With good weather, we continued to pick an additional 4.7 tons of a clean second crop between October 27 and November 4. The harvest produced a total of 189 tons, 81 tons from Russian River (Simoni) and 108 tons from Dry Creek (LeBrett). The following is a comparison between 1976 with the Simoni and Guadagni ranches versus 1977 with the Simoni and LeBrett ranches:

Year	Total (tons)	Price per ton, Zinfandel	Price per ton, Pinot Noir	Total Income
1976	58	$360	$300	$20,371
1977	189 (+326%)	$450 (+25%)	$335 (+12%)	$71,950 (+353%)

I was very fortunate because I had been rescued from what could have been a disastrous year. The year's promising early beginnings were diminished by record drought and heat, only to be rejuvenated by miracle pre-harvest rains. Although the Dry Creek crop of 108 tons was below the 150-ton average that had been shared with me prior to my acquisition of the property, the crop and income totals were personal highs for me as a winegrower. Total operating expense for the year on both vineyards was $38,670, yielding a profit of $33,280. My decision to expand operations was off to a good start, and I was confident I was on the right track.

After harvest, I removed 4.25 acres of old vine Zinfandel at Dry Creek that was planted 8' × 8' on a steep 35% slope. Cultivation by tractor was hard work and time-consuming because a small vineyard tractor could only cultivate downhill. Carrying grape-filled wooden lug boxes up and down these slopes was hard on the harvest crew. The old vines were removed with a small bulldozer that had a crowfoot attachment mounted on the blade to lift and push out the vines. I planned to replant a 7' × 12' terraced vineyard with 3' berms to allow a level 9' row for tractor operations. The site was then ripped 24" deep to break up hardpan, and surface roots were removed by hand. However, ripping the soil would prove to be a huge mistake because the later heavy winter rains caused considerable erosion.

Because of the record low rainfall for the year, it was also a good time to clean out the Dry Creek shallow pond that was now nearly dry, and remove surrounding tule clumps, brush, tree limbs, and sediment. For this task, I employed the same neighbor and equipment that had been used to pull the vines. Even though I had no immediate plans for using the pond, it would be good to take advantage of the opportune conditions to clean it out in advance of winter rain.

The replanting in Dry Creek and improvements to the Dry Creek pond were the first projects in a major reconstruction program on both ranches that would span the next 15 years.

CHAPTER 6

Reconstruction

AFTER I ACQUIRED THE LEBRETT RANCH in 1977, the years of 1978-1995 became a period of reconstruction. As far as I was concerned this was going to be it. I saw no need to acquire additional vineyard property that would require more work and expense, just for the sake of earning greater income. I was determined to make it on what had been acquired to date. If there would be any thoughts of getting bigger, I thought someday it might be desirable to have a small winery on the property to make estate wines from the vineyard. A winery was a beautiful dream, but, in reality, it was low priority because my immediate goals were to replant my older vineyards to premium varietals of higher value, maintain my better blocks of older Zinfandel, make capital improvements on the two properties we owned . . . , and last, but not least, provide for my family of five.

Replanting Vineyard Blocks

The reconstruction period involved removing various blocks of old vine Zinfandel, Carignane, Petite Sirah, French Colombard, and Burger vines from both the Dry Creek (DC) and Russian River Valley (ORH) ranches. Older blocks, where vines were removed, were replanted to premium varietals. Some of the better blocks of old vine Zinfandel and Carignane were maintained in production, as shown in table below.

	Russian River Ranch (ORH)		**Dry Creek (DC)**	
Planted (acres)	Pinot Noir Chardonnay	5.4 8.2	Sauvignon Blanc Chardonnay Cabernet Sauvignon	8.0 2.0 10.0
Maintained (acres)	Old Vine Zinfandel	8.4	Old Vine Zinfandel Carignane	15.0 2.0
Total Bearing (acres)	33.0		37.0	

All the new plantings were planted on wire trellis with drip irrigation. Vine spacing of 8' × 8' was changed to 7' × 12' and 6.4' × 10' to provide wider rows for tractors, and to make vineyard management easier.

Trellised Cabernet Sauvignon, Dry Creek Ranch, looking west.

During the reconstruction period, bearing acreage varied at any given time from 59 to 45 acres. Average annual production was 196 tons/year. Highest production was 243 tons in

1979; lowest was 162 tons in 1984. Grapes could be first harvested three years after planting, and, normally, with an initial yield of about one ton per acre.

During this reconstruction period, grape prices generally rose in Sonoma County. Average base prices per ton for our premium varietals are compared below:

	1978	1995
Sauvignon Blanc	$730	$810
Chardonnay	$862	$1,208
Pinot Noir	$389	$1,194
Cabernet Sauvignon	$516	$1,263

We received a high of $1,365/ton for both Chardonnay and Cabernet in 1993.

Rising prices for Zinfandel over the reconstruction period were also noteworthy. Sonoma County average base prices per ton grew steadily:

	1978–1984	1985–1991	1992–1995
Zinfandel	$434	$737	$950

Zinfandel pricing was $650/ton in 1987, and we were able to sell second-crop Zinfandel at $425/ton, a notably high price for second crop grapes. This high price was driven by the boom in sales of White Zinfandel wine, which was quickly becoming popular. This wine was low in alcohol, slightly sweet, refreshing to drink, and sold at an attractive price. In 1988 and 1989, we were paid an amazing $1,000/ton for Zinfandel, and we received $650/ton for our second crop. In 1994 we received a high of $1,100/ton for Dry Creek Zinfandel.

In 1992, I had planted two acres of Zinfandel on a drip irrigated trellis with the objective of trying to obtain similar quality between dry-farmed old Zinfandel vines and young vines planted on a trellis with irrigation. There was a huge disparity in price between the two, because wineries paid a lower price for young Zinfandel, thinking it to be of lesser quality. However, growing vines on trellis was desirable for vineyard management because it was less physically demanding on the pickers, wider row spacing allowed for tractor work, and *cordon pruning* led to higher production. With *cordons*, the vine would have almost twice the number of production buds as the old vine head-pruned Zinfandel. To achieve parity in flavor between old and new vines, vine parameters were maintained as consistently as possible. The new vine spacing would be 6.4' × 10' (64 square feet per vine), similar to 64 square feet per vine of the old vines on 8' × 8' spacing. We used St. George root stock budded with the old vine clone from our vineyard to maintain the same plant parentage. Soil, climate, and *situs* between the old and new Zinfandel vineyard were the same because the new block was planted adjacent to the old block. For the trellis, a V-shaped bar, similar in style to a rabbit-ear TV antenna, was fastened to each stake supporting five wires for vertical shoot positioning. With proper canopy management, leaf pulling in the fruit zone, drip irrigation, thinning, and a slightly delayed harvest, we proved we could get twice the production using this system versus the old vine head-pruned system. Of greater importance, on a blind tasting of fruit, you couldn't taste any difference in flavors between the old vine and the new. Prices paid for fruit from the trellised new Zinfandel, in some cases, even exceeded the price paid on the older vines.

Starting in 1994, we used this basic V-design to retrofit 2-wire trellis systems that had been installed with wooden stakes. After that year, we went to steel stakes with the V-bars field-welded to the stakes when installing future trellis systems.

It was always difficult for me to remove old vines from the vineyard because I had grown to love them. I had a lot of respect for them. I often wondered about these old vines planted so many years ago. What stories could these vintage vines tell of their hardships in bearing fruit while enduring cold, frost, low rainfall, and blistering summer heat? I admired how they had survived an off-course tractor driver who had bumped them and broken their extended arms, or how they had been knocked down only to be propped up again. Or how they had been reconstructed from a small emerging sucker. These old vines had an internal immune system all their own. They were not susceptible to the viruses and diseases that commonly affected the fickle premium varietals such as Cabernet, Chardonnay, and Pinot Noir.

Old Vine Zinfandel in winter, the Grand Dames of the Vineyard, Dry Creek Ranch.

Being among the old Zinfandel vines in the solitude of winter was like being in a sacred cathedral. It seemed you could quietly meditate and communicate with them. They would tell you what they needed as they revealed their nakedness, devoid of leaves and canopy. You would respond by giving them the tuck and trim they needed with your pruning shears and saw. I cherished pruning these old vines. It was like constructing a work of art, and I got great satisfaction shaping them. They were the magnificent grand dames of the vineyard who became like family to me. Every year they would pass in review as I moved through the vineyard on my tractor. Some of them maintained a perfect voluptuous shape, elegantly poised and well-proportioned with 8-10 arms in an upward open goblet form. Others were not as fortunate, as evident from missing parts, split trunks, or irregular bent shape. Most of them stood erect without a stake. They needed no wire trellis to carry the weight of their fruit. They stood proud year after year, and with care and good weather they could deliver a modest crop of 2-3 tons/acre. I hated myself whenever I did tractor damage to any of these old vines. I was often asked how many years these old vines would continue to produce a viable crop. To me they were like old growth redwood trees. I believed they would continue to produce provided they were pruned judiciously and were given proper nutrients and care.

Selling Grapes to Gallo

A humorous incident happened during the harvest of 1978. After the difficulties we had had with two wineries in 1974 (Seghesio and Souverain), all our production since 1975 had been going to Gallo/Frei Bros. The Gallo winery was the major buyer for most grapes produced in Sonoma County's Dry Creek Valley, but Gallo also brought in grapes from the Alexander and Russian River Valleys and from Mendocino County. At the peak of harvest there would be a long line of trucks and trailers loaded with grapes that would extend from the Gallo sugar stand in Dry Creek Valley far as 200 yards towards Dry Creek Road. The line would move slowly towards the crush pad as sugar tests had to be conducted on all loads being delivered. There could be delays caused by trucks not starting because of dead batteries, vapor locked engines, or problems hooking up cables to dump into the receiving hopper from a variety of trailer configurations, gondolas, and bins. During these delays, growers would get out of their trucks and congregate to talk about the harvest, the weather, and everything else under the sun.

It was routine for Mr. Julio Gallo to visit the winery on a weekly basis to inspect operations and meet with winery personnel. He would arrive by private helicopter from Modesto and would be accompanied by three or four VIPs. He liked coming to the winery during harvest. He could have passed as one of the growers, dressed as he was in khaki work clothes and sporting a baseball-style field hat. When hearing the chop-chop-chop of the helicopter rotor blades in the distance, growers knew Gallo was approaching. Everyone would quickly break up their conversations, tidy up their loads, get back in their truck, and look serious.

After passing through the sugar stand with a five-ton load of ripe Zinfandel grapes heaped high, I was about eight trucks from unloading. I got out of the truck and was standing by the receiving hopper observing the conveyor process, when I happened to look back over my shoulder and saw Mr. Gallo heading for my truck. He climbed up on the running board of my 1947 Chevy flatbed, gave a look at my load then stepped down and went looking for the Gallo grower representative, Rick Buchignani. He asked Rick, "Whose truck is that?" Rick replied "That's Forchini!" Gallo then asked "What's he got on?" Rick came over to me to ask, "What's on your load?" I replied, "Zinfandel." Rick went back to Gallo and said, "Forchini is delivering Zinfandel." Upon hearing this, Gallo led Rick to my truck, pointed to an unusual cluster positioned high on the top of my load, and asked Rick to retrieve it. Rick struggled to climb from the running board up on the flatbed and reached far over the gondola side to retrieve the unusual cluster that Gallo had spotted.

The guilty cluster was a huge three-pound bunch of Black Moscato grapes that came from an old vine that had been interplanted in the vineyard. In the early days, it was not uncommon to interplant a few other varieties such as Alicante, Petite Sirah, or Carignane with Zinfandel to get a field blend for red wine. The difference in appearance between a bunch of Black Moscato and Zinfandel is obvious. Zinfandel's main cluster is elongated with loose, medium-sized berries; it is a small shoulder cluster and red magenta in color. Black Moscato has a large, compact oval cluster, three times the weight of a Zinfandel cluster, with huge, round berries that are dark black in color. Give Mr. Gallo an "A" for grape identification! Black Moscato is delicious to eat, and it was obvious a picker had cut off a bunch to eat, took a few bites, then tossed the bunch on top of the load. In general, whenever I saw an odd bunch of a different variety coming in, I would bury it in a corner of the gondola loaded with Zinfandel.

Gallo wanted to make sure I wasn't misrepresenting my load because the price differential between Zinfandel and mixed black grapes was great. He stayed close by and made me a nervous wreck, knowing that he could reject my load in a second and send me "down the road" with a full gondola searching for a home. As my gondola was hoisted and dumped into the hopper, Gallo was there watching closely, backed up by his entourage of VIPs. At an angle of about 50 degrees, grapes began to fall from the gondola and Gallo could inspect my large load of loose clustered fruit which blanketed the hopper screw conveyer. After tasting a berry or two of this sweet, fruity and spicy fruit, he was convinced my load was truly Zinfandel. He looked at me, nodded his head, and, with a wink of his eye in satisfaction, walked away, giving me a sense of relief. My cold sweat was over! I didn't mind Gallo's hands-on scrutiny. . . . In fact I admired it. What a man he was!

As part of our 1979 harvest, we did a special 40-ton order of Zinfandel from Dry Creek for a small Bay Area winery. They wanted to crush in the vineyard immediately as each bucket was picked. They came with a crusher mounted on a flatbed truck, and they pumped the *must* directly to a tank trailer for transport back to their winery. They made two round trips within a period of 48 hours to transport 6,600 gallons of juice. They thought this was better than trucking 40 tons of fruit a distance of 80 miles to their winery, and then crushing the fruit three hours later. It was an interesting project and it saved me eight round trips to Gallo.

I had a very good relationship with the Gallo winery through the years. They had always treated me well, having picked me up after my being thrown out of Souverain and losing Seghesio in 1974. Gallo would give growers an advanced payment of up to 40% of what had been delivered to help with harvest expenses. Gallo always paid in full before the end of the year, and gave generous presents of wine and brandy at Christmas.

Dealing With Changing Climate

In 1984, the local paper started to pay attention to climate change. The weather was getting weird, and it was reported that El Niño was partially to blame. It was either too wet or too dry, and triple digit heat seemed to be more frequent. Normal marine layers of fog, which cooled the Northern California coastline during summer months, were inconsistent. The drought years of 1976–1977, followed by 63" of rain in 1978, was another warning of future weather abnormalities. Accumulated rainfall for Sonoma County was usually around 40", and was measured between July 1 and June 30 of the following year. In 1980, we had five days of 100–107°F heat during harvest, and in August 1981 before harvest, days of 102°F and 105°F. In May 1982, we had accumulated 63" of rain. Experts were saying the period 1983–84 was the warmest two-year period since the California Gold Rush 135 years before, and nine out of 20 days in September of 1883 were above 100°F. In May 1983, we had accumulated 83", which was the heaviest rainfall on record, followed by 3" during harvest that ruined 35 tons of grapes. In May 1987, we had temperatures of 100°F, 102° F, and 100°F. In 1988, only 3" of rain was received by April, followed by three days above 100°F in August. In 1989, we had below-freezing temperatures in February (18°F, 12°F, 15°F, and 18°F), and in September we were greeted with thunder, lightning, and 5" of rain that caused power failures and delayed the start of harvest. In 1990, we received 6" of rain in May, which was the highest total ever recorded for May. In January 1991, we again had below-freezing temperatures over a two-week period that sent temperatures dropping to 15–20°F. By April 1993, we had received 46" of rain to date, making it the heaviest rainfall to that date in seven years. This was followed by a wet and muggy spring with heavy rain on Memorial Day, and more rain in June.

Mother Nature could be good or bad. Abnormality now seemed to be the norm. I hated triple digit heat at any time throughout the growing season. It was very hard on my large number of dry-farmed old vine Zinfandel plants, although above-normal rain was stored away like money in the bank by these same vines.

ORH Improvements

In 1984, work began on a large project with the U.S. Soil Conservation Service, to improve the drainage through our vineyard at ORH. Together, we developed an above-ground drainage ditch 10' wide and 1,400' in length with two inlet catch basins that drained runoff accumulating from U.S. 101 highway and the hillside watersheds from Limerick Lane to the east. The ditch was seeded with Blando Brome grass to help slow the water velocity and help keep the soil beneath the grass dry enough that you could cross it in the spring by tractor. The advantages of this new waterway were numerous. It replaced 525' of a heavily silted 24" buried concrete pipe, and 875' of an open ditch that ran through the vineyard. This was a huge improvement because at times of heavy rains, our property would flood in the lower regions and delay necessary tractor work until late spring. The grass waterway also allowed additional plantings of vines on both sides because it eliminated the wide spaces needed to turn tractors unable to cross the former open ditch. The old ditch was a nightmare of weeds, silt, and debris, and it required constant maintenance.

At the end of the 1986 harvest, I was disappointed with the low production of only 50 and 44 tons that had been harvested at ORH. I considered selling the vineyard. It was something I really did not want to do, but I was getting a little worn out with all the projects, moving equipment, and balancing harvests between two vineyards. I thought ORH had appreciated in value, and I could put some money in the bank that would be used for projects at Dry Creek; in addition, it would make my life a little easier.

In October 1987, I placed a "For Sale By Owner" ad in the local newspaper, and on a whim asked $580,000. I offered the sale to various realtor friends on a non-exclusive basis. I received 56 inquiries from interested buyers and a high offer for $690,000. This told me the demand for my vineyard property was high and worth a lot more than I had realized. My offer to sell had served as an appraisal of the value of the property. I decided not to sell "short," but rather to continue with what I was doing. My health was good, and at the age of 48, I believed I still had a lot of productive years ahead.

In 1988, I installed an expansive underground network of 3" PVC pipe over the entire ranch, with risers for drip irrigation in the newly planted vineyard blocks. At other strategic locations, a PVC riser with valve and fitting was provided to connect with laterals of portable aluminum pipe for irrigating the older head-pruned Zinfandel. Using pull hoses attached to the laterals, self-supporting, 4'-high impulse sprinklers could be placed anywhere in the vineyard, which didn't need to be tied off with twine to adjacent vines. Moving through a muddy vineyard with heavy 20' sections of 3" pipe attached with fixed sprinklers was hard work. To my joy, Anita could help move the pull hose system. But she declined to move the 20' pipe sections. . . . She would forego that adventure and chose housework instead.

After the harvest of 1988, we took a winter vacation on November 30 to visit our daughter, Carla, in Lima, Peru, where she was spending her third year at Humboldt State University as a Spanish major. Anita and I, along with our youngest son, Andrew, went to visit her over the Christmas holidays. We stopped over in Dallas, Texas, to see our older son, Michael, who was working for a large manufacturer, producing fencing panels for big box retailers. In our absence, I authorized Transito, an employee who lived in the rented house on our DC property with his wife, to start pruning there on November 30 and keep an eye on the ranch. He was to work 9 hours/day, 6 days/week and would be self-supervised. He had worked for me the past year after moving in. He was a man of good character, could prune well, and I trusted him. He was to be joined on weekends by two brothers who had pruned for me part-time in the past. On January 2, 1989, we returned from Peru. I hired more pruners to finish Dry Creek and start pruning at ORH. Things had worked out during our absence. Only four acres remained for pruning at DC, and everything looked to be in good order; by March 14 we had completed pruning at ORH.

In 1991, I was approached by a realtor friend, who had been involved in the former non-exclusive sale "evaluation" of ORH in 1987. He asked if I might again be interested in listing my ORH property for sale. He suggested a sales price of $830,000. This potential gain of $765,000 minus taxes and selling costs would be a nice little nest egg to drop in the bank, and at 53 I could live an easier life in Dry Creek. I signed an exclusive agreement with the realtor to sell, and soon received three interested buyers. Again, I was caught in a dilemma: Did I really want to sell when grape prices were increasing? Of equal importance, I did have two sons who had potential in the winegrowing industry: Andrew was showing interest in the vineyards, and Michael had production and sales experience which might contribute to a future winery someday. So, once again, I decided to take ORH off the market and continue with what I had been doing. I was in very good health, which I attributed to outdoor physical activity. So, why sell?

A New Home

During the reconstruction period I spent very little money on the old original house at Dry Creek, which I had been renting to various parties. The house was in poor condition, and I was prepared to take it down at some future time. We had kept the ranch house at ORH in good condition, having lived in it for nine years. But as of May 1979, I realized I was going to be 41 years old; Anita would be 38, and Michael, Carla, and Andrew would be 14, 12, and 5. We weren't going to be able to live in that one-bathroom old ranch house at ORH much longer. We needed a new home with more room and conveniences, or there was going to be a major revolt.

Completed house at Dry Creek home ranch, viewed from west, showing porch along front wall, ca. 1980.

Anita and I sketched out some floor plans that ended up being a two-story house which included 3,000 square feet living area, four bedrooms, three baths, dining room, living room, family room, laundry room, and attached garage. The plan also included my custom design for a 210 square foot, copper-paneled, hot water solar system mounted under glass, on the garage roof facing south. Hot water was a valuable commodity for our family as Anita was always running the washing machine filled with clothes from vineyard work, school, play, and dress. With an abundance of wood available on the property from pruning vines and downed trees, two airtight wood-fired stoves were incorporated for interior heating.

I began work on the preparations for a set of building plans, and after many trips to the Sonoma County Planning Department, my plans with markups and redline corrections were approved for building. We took out a small construction loan from Production Credit, a local farmer-friendly loan agency, with payments to be made after harvest. Construction began in August on an elevated site above the vineyard.

I was heavily involved in the building project. I did all the procurement and subcontracting, delivered materials, assisted in construction where possible, and closely followed plan compliance. It soon became apparent that the contractor and I didn't get along very well, and we had a falling out. He quit after we got to the main floor. He didn't like me being so involved, thought engineers didn't know anything about construction, and wanted to use his favorite suppliers, not the ones I had selected. As for me, I didn't like some of his construction methods or some of his suggestions to save costs that I believed compromised the design. So, it was a mutual parting of the ways. And it was also a good time to pause house construction, because harvest was fast approaching.

By late July in 1980, we were ready for interior finishing work on the new house. Anita and I did all the interior painting, installed the wallpaper, and my brother and I installed pre-finished hardwood flooring and stairs. We moved out of the ORH ranch house and into our new home in August, which was 95% finished on the interior minus some moldings and trim. However, the house was surrounded by the dismal aftermath of construction; it was a landscape of bare excavated dirt, used lumber and various construction debris. Not an attractive site on that hot, exposed, sundrenched knoll. However, we were eager to get established in our new home, and we knew that, in time, with landscaping it would become a beautiful homesite. There was a resident community of rattlesnakes living in the area with whom we struggled over territorial rights, and I became adept at reducing their population. They were not an endangered species. . . . We were the endangered species.

Dry Creek Ranch home site on knoll. Showing garage with solar water system on roof at left, house and pool at center, and gardens to right. (Based on present-day satellite map by Google Map GIS. Annotations by editor)

Other Projects

In addition to replanting the vineyards and building our new home, many other improvement projects were undertaken during this reconstruction period that added to my vineyard management work.

After the initial cleaning of the pond in 1978 (mentioned in the preceding chapter), I developed a plan with the help of the U.S. Soil Conservation Service to increase the capacity of the shallow pond to 2.6 acre-feet, by building a small dam with an underground culvert to handle a 50-year storm. A road was constructed across the top of the dam that went 500' upwards on a gentle grade to the site of our new home (discussed in the previous pages).

After the harvest of 1979, we drilled an 8" well below the new house site at a location adjacent to the seasonal creek that flowed towards the pond. The location had not been witched; it was chosen based on the contractor's experience and recommendations. After drilling and testing at a depth of 300' the well delivered only 5 gpm. So, I hired an old local water witcher (also called a "dowser") who had a history of locating water in Dry Creek Valley. He said without hesitation, the location where we were drilling was a bad choice, and he suggested we move downstream to a better site he had discovered based on a strong pull on his witching rod. Rather than continue to drill deeper at that current location the contractor had recommended, I made the decision to pull the casing and re-drill at the new location the witcher was suggesting.

Maybe it was my intuition that sided with that underground force that pulled against the dowser's conductive rod. Maybe it was the self-confidence of that old man who recommended that I pull the casing and change location. Or maybe it was the good result I had from witching the well at ORH years earlier. Whatever, after pulling 15 pieces of 20-foot casing and moving the drilling rig to the new location, we drilled down until . . . *Eureka!* . . . we found water that tested 40 gpm at a level of 130', which dropped only 10' after four hours of testing. The old dowser was right, and I felt good that I had respected his judgment, even though it added to the expense of the well. Based on this test result, we installed a 7½ hp pump at a depth of 210', that delivered 50 gpm against a 400' head. This would be adequate for vineyard drip irrigation in blocks of 6 acres, and provide 60 psi pressure at the new house that was located 100' above the well site.

In 1978 after harvest, knowing that I would be doing a lot of future vineyard development, I built a hydraulic stake press (driver) that delivered 12 tons of force when powered by the external hydraulics of the tractor. The press could be attached and removed from the side of my crawler tractor and could be adjusted to accommodate stakes from 5-7' in length. This would be a good tool to have, since it eliminated the hard labor required to drive stakes by hand, or the need to hire a contractor to do this work.

In early 1980, I also replaced a ½ hp, 10 gpm submersible pump at the pond with a 1½ hp, 16 gpm pump, which would be adequate for drip irrigation in blocks for the new plantings of Sauvignon Blanc and Chardonnay at Dry Creek.

In 1989, I built a sickle-bar cane trimmer to trim canopies on my trellised vineyards. This device could be adjusted for row width and blade angle, and each side could be individually raised or lowered to work on terraced vineyards. This cane trimmer saved a lot of hand labor required to trim canopies, allowing sunlight into the fruit zone. Opening the canopy helped prevent mildew, reduced fungicide applications, and enhanced berry color.

In 1990, I bought some rejected roof trusses at a bargain price from the same company that had made trusses for our new house. I designed a 21' × 31' floor plan for a barn structure that would use these odd trusses. Two 10'-wide covered side bays were added on each side of the new barn to provide tractor shelter and a pump house to cover the well that supplied water to the old ranch house. With the help of vineyard workers, we dismantled the old barn, and, joined by our older son, Michael, and two of his friends, we built a new barn with a roll-up door on a concrete slab. The new barn had space for two tractors and included a work bench, electrical service for a welder, and storage bins for parts and fittings.

The 1995 Harvest

The harvest of 1995 produced a crop of 191 tons, which produced a record income of over $4,300/acre on 54 bearing acres. With the completion of harvest in mid-October, I quickly planted crimson clover cover crops in the trellised vineyard blocks at both Dry Creek and Russian River, hoping to catch some early rain. But as luck would have it, the weather remained warm, dry and frost free, which allowed the vines to stubbornly hold on to a straggled canopy of crimson, faded green, and yellow leaves. This canopy attracted lots of birds to feast on bunches of second-crop grapes that had shriveled to raisins, and on the scattered clover seed on the ground. Finally, on December 1, it started to rain, and my cover crop germinated. I looked forward to getting some rest for the holidays and to a beautiful carpet of bright crimson clover flowers the following spring. With rain pounding on the roof, and in a melancholy mood, sitting by a cozy fire, I started to contemplate building that special winery which had been in the back of our minds ever since Bruce and I first made wine in 1969, and I picked my first grapes in 1971. I was 57 years old and not getting any younger. I realized we had best make a decision about a winery soon.

Industry Associations

I should go no further without writing about my involvement with industry associations: the California North Coast Grape Growers Association (CNCGGA) which was established in 1963, the larger statewide California Association of Winegrape Growers (CAWG) established in 1974, and the Sonoma County Grape Growers Association (SCGGA) established in 1983.

In August of 1990, I was elected to serve two years as president of the CNCGGA of which I had been a member since 1971, and I had served on the Board of Directors for the prior three years. CNCGGA was founded by a small group of grape growers from Napa, Sonoma, and Mendocino counties to represent grape growers, primarily on issues related to pricing and contracts in a marketplace dominated by a few large wineries. The Board, which consisted of three members from each of the founding counties, met monthly. In 1990 the Board voted to include new membership from the North Coast counties of Lake, Mendocino, and Marin in addition to the original founding counties. With an expanded membership, CNCGGA became a major and respected influence in the North Coast wine grape industry. CNCGGA provided grape growers with information and direction through regular newsletters, marketing seminars, industrial trade shows, wine school sessions, annual meetings, and banquets. At the annual meetings, CNCGGA would recommend pricing for major red and white grape varietals grown in Napa, Sonoma, and Mendocino counties, in addition to aggregating estimates on grape crop production tonnage by county. Production projections and recommended prices were developed through the Board's monthly meetings, where Board members reported on their discussions with other growers in their district regarding what they were experiencing on market demand, pricing, contracts, and crop levels by varietal. The CNCGGA-recommended pricing became highly respected as a starting point for negotiation. In many cases, CNCGSA pricing was written into contracts between growers and wineries.

Aside from pricing and contracts, CNCGGA also addressed issues on farm labor housing, mechanical harvesting, vineyard operating costs, and the damage to vineyards currently being caused by *Phylloxera*-B on new vineyards planted on *AXR* rootstock. There was also a growing anti-alcohol movement developing with legislation at both national and state levels. They proposed to increase taxes on wine from one cent to $1.28 a gallon, and the infamous "nickel a drink" proposal for a 5-cent tax on a 5-ounce glass of wine served in restaurants. We opposed this tax, and with strong support and lobbying from the Wine Institute and other wine industry participants, we worked to get it defeated.

An additional concern for CNCGGA at this time was the growing membership of CAWG, who had been persistent over many years in their desire to bring in other grape grower organizations under their umbrella. Their objective was to provide a larger statewide leadership for grape growers on political, public, and trade issues through strength in numbers, thus developing a strong voice for all grape growers in California. CNCGGA was worried about the impact that this broader, state-wide association might have on our Sonoma County growers. There was also concern about proposed wine grape commissions that were being encouraged by CAWG.

In 1984, a CAWG marketing order had been approved, that was created jointly by grape growers and vintners to promote California wines by assessing a 1% fee on all grape production. In 1987, there was a proposal to renew this market order in the form of a formal CAWG commission that would be a joint venture of growers and vintners. Renewal of the order would require a separate vote of approval from both groups. The commission did not get the required participation from the vintners, and as a result the market order was terminated in June 1987.

In 1991, during my second term as president, CNCGGA led the fight to oppose a different wine grape commission that was now being proposed by SCGGA to promote Sonoma County wines. SCGGA's message was that by promoting Sonoma County wines, the demand for Sonoma County grapes would increase and would result in higher prices paid to Sonoma County growers. This was not a joint venture of growers and vintners, but rather a grower-only assessment on growers' income to promote Sonoma County wines. There was no provision by this commission for wineries to contribute to this general fund. It was suggested that an increase in winery sales would increase wine grape demand, resulting in higher prices paid to growers. CNCGGA's position was that prices paid to Sonoma County grape growers had been rising without a commission, and that any commission should be a joint effort, including both growers and wineries. In the four years between 1987 and 1990, the Sonoma County average base price paid for Pinot Noir had increased 53% from $531/ton to $810/ton; Cabernet had increased 80% from $707 to $1,275; Chardonnay had increased 36% from $944 to $1,284; and Zinfandel had increased 40% from $520 to $727. Of equal importance, there were established trade groups promoting Sonoma County wines such as the Sonoma County Wineries Association, the Wine Road, various Sonoma County AVA winegrower associations from Dry Creek, Russian River, Alexander, and Sonoma valleys, and the Sonoma County Harvest Fair Board. The Sonoma County Fair Board hosted the prestigious Sonoma County Professional Wine Competition that brought in wine judges from all over the country, to judge and spread the word on the fine wines being produced in Sonoma County. After a 60-day referendum, the wine grape commission failed to get the required votes needed, and as a result, the commission itself failed.

Prior to my term as President, CNCGGA had made the misguided decision in 1977 to buy the Chateau Souverain Winery in Geyserville. This impressive winery was built in 1972 by the Pillsbury Family of Minnesota, known for their Pillsbury flour brand. Pillsbury hired Lee Stewart, the successful winemaker of Napa Valley fame, as consulting winemaker. After a few years of operation, the Pillsburys, who were in red ink, decided the wine business was not for them and put the property up for sale. CNCGGA thought they could make Souverain a success, and offered limited partnerships to grape growers who would not only become part owners of this beautiful winery overlooking Alexander Valley, but also would have the opportunity for a guaranteed home for their grapes dependent upon the amount each grower invested. This sounded good to many growers, who at that time were struggling with securing buyers and contracts. I passed on this opportunity because I had recently bought the LeBrett property and had no interest in investing in anything other than my two vineyards. As fate would have it, after 10 years of operation under CNCGGA control, the Souverain winery suffered the same problems as it had under Pillsbury ownership, and the winery was sold to Berringer, owned by Nestle/Wine World Estates. Those CNCGGA members who had invested as limited partners became disgruntled after losing a substantial amount on their investment. Many of them dropped their membership in CNCGGA in protest.

The loss of these members, coupled with the growing memberships of CAWG and the SCGGA organizations, posed a threat to the future of CNCGGA. The CAWG was mainly representing grape growers from the San Joaquin Valley areas of Lodi, Madera, and Fresno, but the association had also made inroads into the Sierra foothill districts, Paso Robles, Lake County, and Mendocino County. CAWG had, in turn, pushed hard for the formation of SCGGA. However, CNCGGA wanted to remain separate from the larger statewide CAWG, because we believed the North Coast was a premier winegrowing region and should have a separate identity.

North Coast growers, on average, received the highest grape prices paid in California. As an example, grape growers of Sonoma County in 1990 received an average price of $1,284/ton for Chardonnay, $727 for Zinfandel, and $1,275 for Cabernet, whereas San Joaquin Valley areas received a much lower average price of $691/ton for Chardonnay, $279 for Zinfandel, and $522 for Cabernet. San Joaquin growers could also choose among other markets, growing wine grapes not only for cheaper jug wines, but also for table grapes, raisins, and grape concentrate for fruit-flavored beverages. For the San Joaquin growers, large grape production in the order of 10 to 12 tons per acre was possible, but at lower sugar levels. North Coast growers were not engaged in that market, nor did they want to be. This was all the more reason to maintain a separate identity and be recognized as a prestigious growing region for the production of premium red and white table wines.

Even with a declining membership, CNCGGA continued to set recommended pricing for grape growers based on crop estimates and market demand, and to be a voice on North Coast grower issues. But by 2006 the membership of CNCGGA had declined to 20 members, from a high of 700 in 1985. The membership decline was mainly due to the bad aftermath of the Souverain experience, but also on account of a growing SCGGA. Many CNCGGA members from Sonoma County were torn between staying loyal to CNCGGA, or becoming members of this new county-based SCGGA. In August 2006, CNCGGA membership finally voted to disband and allowed their membership to move to CAWG and SCGGA. In tribute to CNCGGA, this original grower organization could stand proudly for the stewardship and accomplishments they had provided for North Coast grape growers over the past 43 years.

With the guidance and persistence of CAWG, and SCGGA now firmly in place, there was a renewed attempt in 2006 to get a wine grape commission started for the purpose of promoting Sonoma County wines. Since I had been involved in the defeat of such a commission in 1991, when I was president of CNCGGA, I was consulted by many of the proponents for this new commission to get my support. I remained a strong advocate for a unified joint commission comprising both growers and wineries with both contributing. However, this new 2006 commission was structured for growers only to be taxed on their grapes sold to wineries, while exempting wineries from contributing to the commission in any manner, unless a winery sold estate grapes to another winery. It was true that wineries were spending dollars on promotion, but these were larger wineries promoting their own brand through media and advertising. The majority of the wineries in Sonoma County only promoted their own brand through their websites and public tasting trade events; they did not spend money to promote Sonoma County wines through the media. This new commission would also exempt grape growers marketing 25 tons or less from paying any assessment. This was disturbing, because there were many growers in Sonoma County who would benefit but would not have to contribute. Those growers marketing 25 tons could easily receive incomes of $30-50,000, depending on the varietal, and at the proposed assessment rate of 0.5%, this would have amounted to a meaningful contribution of $125-250 to the commission fund.

Under the new commission, the SCGGA would be disbanded, leaving grape growers without sole representation. SCGGA would be replaced by the Sonoma County Winegrowers Association, where the primary objectives would be marketing and public relations. As far as I was concerned, this wine grape commission was not structured properly. Growers were being assessed to promote the wines of Sonoma County, while wineries and small growers were exempted. In my opinion this was wrong. I was portrayed as being against promotion, but nothing could have been farther from the truth. I was a member of the Wine Institute, the Sonoma County Wine Road, the Russian River Winegrowers, the Dry Creek Winegrowers, Sonoma County Winery Association, a former member of CNCGGA, Zinfandel Advocate Producers and Family Winemakers. My dues for every one of these organizations went towards promotion of Sonoma County wines.

Proponents for the new wine grape commission presented an argument that portrayed Sonoma County as a "lightweight" when it came to promotional spending. They claimed Sonoma County was spending a paltry $500,000 for promotion, whereas Napa County was spending over $4 million, and other areas such as Oregon, Washington, and Paso Robles were spending well over $1 million each. This was totally false and in error for several reasons. First, the Sonoma County Winery Association (SCWA) would spend well over $500,000 alone to promote Sonoma County wines featuring all the Sonoma County AVAs at their annual *Taste of Sonoma* event in the summer. In addition, SCWA traveled nationally to provide an annual promotional *Grand Tour of Sonoma County* wines in major market areas from coast to coast. Second, the Wine Road would spend thousands promoting Sonoma County wines through their annual special public tasting events (Barrel Tasting, Wine & Food, and Winter Wineland). Third, the Dry Creek Winegrowers alone spent over $500,000 at their annual Passport event; other AVA trade organizations were spending thousands to promote their individual Sonoma County appellations. And lastly, the Sonoma County Harvest Fair Board would spend thousands of dollars for a three-day period of trade and public tastings, promoting all the winning wines from the annual Sonoma County Professional Wine Competition, held annually at the Sonoma County Fairgrounds.

To suggest that Sonoma County was only spending $500,000 in promotion was grossly misleading and preposterous. Either no one wanted to correctly add up all the dollars being spent, or someone had failed in math. It was equally disappointing that leaders of the various Sonoma County trade organizations and the Harvest Fair Board did not publicly speak out, and be counted as to how much they were each spending towards hosting promotional events. For some reason they choose to remain silent. Growers alone would be the ones forced to raise over $1.2 million through an assessment on their grape sales to establish the Sonoma County Winegrape Commission, without any contributions from wineries or any other related businesses that would benefit from increased sales of Sonoma County wines. After a short period of lobbying by the proponents, the commission proposal was set for a vote by the registered grape growers of Sonoma County.

There was a 60-day referendum period that required 40% of all eligible Sonoma County grape growers to vote for or against this new 2006 wine grape commission. After 60 days, the 40% requirement had not been met and the commission should have been defeated. But for some undisclosed reason, the voting period was extended until enough growers had voted to meet the minimum 40% requirement. At that point, it was publicly announced in the local media that over 80% of the growers in Sonoma County voted overwhelmingly in favor of the commission. Unlike the election results of a candidate for public office, the actual numbers of growers voting for or against the commission were never published.

The reality was a much different outcome: Only 65% of the required voting minimum of 40% of the growers were needed to vote in favor of the commission; or, only 51% of this minimum 40% voting block were required to vote in favor, if those 51% marketed 65% or more of the grapes produced in the County. That being the case, but without a full accounting, this means the wine grape commission could have been approved by only 20-26% of the 1,800 growers in Sonoma County. We will never know.

Without question, promotion is essential to our wine industry, and with broader participation, more could have been raised at a lower assessment rate for each participant. It was hard to understand why a unified commission of growers and wineries, working together to create a general fund for the promotion of Sonoma County wines, was not appealing. Knowing how hard grape growers work through the growing season, in addition to being good stewards of the land to promote open space and green belts, it seemed unfair to place a tax only on the growers to promote the Sonoma County wine industry, while others who would benefit from the promotion were exempt. It was not a level playing field!

CHAPTER 7

Winemaking

DURING THE WINTER OF 1996, my thoughts about building a small winery, to produce estate grown and bottled wines that would express the quality of our grapes, began to intensify. I knew our grapes were of high quality because they tasted good when eating them out in the vineyards during harvest. The flavors were rich and deep and lingered on the palatte, and I thought if you could capture these same flavors in the bottle, you could probably produce a delicious wine. I also knew there was greater income potential selling wine rather than just selling grapes.

Conception of a Winery

During this time, a grape grower who sold Zinfandel for $1,100/ton, would get about $500/ton net income after deducting production, depreciation, and interest expenses. If the grape grower bottled wine from that same ton of grapes, about 750 bottles of wine could be produced. If that wine was sold at an average price of $15/bottle, the gross income would be $11,250 per ton. After deducting costs of growing, production, and overhead, the net income could be approximately $10,000, or 20 times more than selling that same ton of grapes. Clearly, it was more lucrative to sell a ton of grapes as bottled wine rather than as delivered fruit. However, two to three years would pass while the wine aged and could be sold, and only after that could the grape grower start to recover his costs, whereas in selling grapes to another wine producer, the grower got paid within three to six months, if not immediately. Another consideration: If the grower sold some of the wine wholesale to retailers and distributors, the net income would be reduced 33-50%. And there was also the risk that the wine might show evidence of defects or spoilage before or after bottling, which would result in some loss of product and income. So, making wine was not without risk.

In 1971 when we started as growers, the US adult per capita wine consumption was a little over two gallons per adult. In California, consumption that same year was 4.8 gallons per adult. By 1980 the adult per capita consumption of wine in California had jumped to 6.3 and was predicted to keep increasing. I recognized that a winery would involve much additional work, beyond that I was already committed to in the vineyard. There would be new things to learn, and additional risk and uncertainty. But Anita and I had experience dealing with uncertainties, and we believed we could meet new challenges. Andrew was soon to graduate from Fresno State, where he was majoring in viticulture, and he could help in the vineyard. Mike and Carla at ages 31 and 29 might also help, although they each had their own careers. Even so, we put no pressure on the kids, or suggested that a decision to go forward with a winery was in any way dependent upon their commitment to help. It was our decision to make and now was the time to make it. Were we going to follow an ambitious dream or discard the whole idea of a winery, only to later regret that we should have proceeded? On a unanimous vote of 2–0, Anita and I made the decision to plan and build a small winery to produce a limited selection of estate grown, produced, and bottled wines.

Dry Creek Winery Site, 2023.
(Based on present-day terrain map by Google Map GIS. Annotations by editor.)

In February I developed preliminary specifications and drawings for a simple winery building. Not knowing how successful our winery might be, I wanted the building to be utilitarian in design so it could easily be used for other purposes, should the winery not work out. All winery equipment would be portable, either mounted on casters or moveable by forklift. Storage tanks would not be supported on concrete benches or on pedestals integrated with the floor. Barrels would be stored on stacked, separable steel racks. The winery would be located on the moderate 11% slope of the upper benchland on our main entrance road, which turned east from Dry Creek Rd. and climbed a gentle 6% grade about 500' to the benchland. The winery would not be visible from Dry Creek Road. I wondered if this would be an advantage or a disadvantage. But it was the only practical location.

The winery building would be 32' × 56' and used for fermenting, wine storage and bottling. The building would include a 12' × 8' lab/office, 6' × 6' lavatory, and stairs leading to a 3'-high, elevated, 14' × 32' crush pad with an adjacent 6' × 6' mechanical room. The winery would have a 10'-high, insulated, roll-up metal door, and a concrete slab floor with drains leading to underground cement storage tanks for process water and sewage. The insulated walls would be 12' high. The ceiling would also be insulated. The exterior wall siding would be stained wood, rough-sawn board and bat; interior walls would be sealed plywood. The hipped roof would be supported by pre-fabricated roof trusses, topped by a louvered 4' × 8' cupola and 42" exhaust fan (3-phase, 220v). Other interior utilities would include 110v electrical outlets, compressed air outlets, fluorescent office lighting, and four high-bay, interior vapor lights. All waste and process water would be pumped from the underground tanks, 300' via underground pipeline, to storage on a knoll above the vineyard for later discharge and surface infiltration.

The building would be classified as commercial, which required that the plans be submitted to an architect for preparation of construction drawings. That cost $1,700. We accepted a construction bid for $63,000 from a building contractor, who happened to be the nephew of former owner Paul LeBrett. The bid was attractive, but did not include sub-contracting for excavation, trusses, electrical, and plumbing. This nephew's low bid might have been influenced by his connection to the property when visiting and playing on the ranch in his younger days.

On March 12, 1996, we applied to the Sonoma County Permit and Resource Management Department for a 3,000-case winery, with tasting-by-appointment, and paid a fee of $1,643. On April 18, a contract was awarded for percolation testing and septic system design for $2,550. Some other minor fees and inspection were required for Public Health permits, Public Works & Roads evaluations, Fire Marshall's inspection, Emergency Services notification and plan, a Cultural Resource Study, and a Sound Study for potential noise abatement. Our winery building permit was approved on May 16. The septic system testing and plans were approved on May 30, 1996.

I started in April to purchase and fabricate equipment that would be needed for making my first wine after the 1996 harvest. My engineering experience was invaluable, allowing me to design and fabricate most of the equipment in our barn shop using an electric-arc, stick welder, abrasive cut-off wheel, drill press, and grinder. Structural steel shapes, angles, and bars were easy to weld; all steel components were primed and painted for protection against corrosion.

Three stainless-steel, 2-ton, open-top, 4'9"-diameter × 4'-high, 530-gallon fermenters were ordered from a local tank manufacturer. Tank stands were designed and built to support a fully loaded tank of 4,300 lbs., 12" above the floor. For a must pump, I purchased a Liverani flexible, rubber-vane pump with 3" ports capable of pumping 30 gpm at a head of 80'. The pump was mounted on a moveable cart, powered by a 2 hp motor with a reversing drum switch. For dumping grapes from harvest bins, I designed and fabricated a steel bin dumper, powered by a 2 hp hydraulic pump and 3" cylinder that could rotate a 1,500 lb. 4' × 4' bin 120 degrees from horizontal. I designed a stainless-steel, pie-shaped, truncated chute to receive the grapes from the bin dumper; I had this fabricated by a local shop because I did not have the capacity to weld stainless steel. To support the chute, I designed and built a steel frame on casters that could be positioned over the crusher at a fixed angle of 30 degrees. At this angle, with a little help from gravity, we could easily drag and gently pull the grapes to feed the crusher. For crushing grapes, I purchased a 2.4 hp Lugana 1 grape separator that could process 4-5 tons/hr. The grape separator knocked the grape berries from the stems by revolving paddles inside a rotating perforated drum yielding a high percentage of whole berries. This process would allow a fermentation process known as *carbonic maceration* where the weight of the berries would gently break grape skins to release juice; as the fermentation proceeded, all the skins would eventually soften and release juice. The objectives behind the selection of the grape separator, carbonic maceration, flexible pump, large ports, and the gravity feed chute would be to minimize the extraction of bitter *tannins* from the stems and seeds. I purchased a Rossi wood-basket press with an internal, inflatable water bladder that could press approximately 3 tons of fermented must. I procured a 3000L (792 gal), stainless-steel Marchisio tank for racking the wine and temporary storage. This would be enough equipment to get started and complete the initial production phases of primary and secondary fermentation.[12]

12 The Liverani, Lugana, Marchisio, and Rossi equipment were all fabricated in Italy and purchased from a local manufacturing representative. Italy has numerous manufacturers of winery equipment designed for small wineries, whereas the availability of such equipment made in the U.S. was very limited. Other European producers of small winery equipment could be found in France, Germany, and Switzerland, but Italy was my favorite go-to country for winery machinery. It is not surprising that Italy's renowned reputation for fashion, automobiles, arms, architecture, music, and art also extended to winery equipment.

Construction started on the main winery building on June 10, after razing the old rental house and completing the excavation for footings and a floor slab. By June 19, the foundation walls and footings had been completed. The performance of the building contractor and his crew was exceptional, and we were in very good hands. This was gratifying and gave me peace of mind because I was busy in the vineyards with cultivation, sulfur dusting, suckering, and fabricating equipment. I didn't want to deal with any bad experiences as when building the house in 1979. By July 26, rough framing and plumbing, hold downs, shear walls, and truss placement had been completed. By August 14, close-in siding, sheathing, sub-roof plywood, rough electrical, stairs, and handrails had been completed. After the rough electrical was installed, and handrails and stairs were completed, we paid $96 and applied for a temporary occupation permit, which allowed for an electric meter to be installed and for the building to be used. The winery building would not receive final sign off until February 11, 1997, but with the temporary occupation permit, we would be able to process grapes starting in the fall of 1996.

First Crush

Since making my first homemade wine with Bruce and Gordon in 1969, I had been studying the principles of winemaking in various publications, to increase my knowledge of the basics and to improve the quality of wines I was making for personal use. On an annual basis, I had been making house wine in the cellars of both the Russian River ranch house and our new Dry Creek home, using second crop grapes left after harvest. Using first crop grapes for house wines was not practical because we were dependent on the income from selling that first crop. My Spartan equipment then, consisted of a hand-crank roller crusher that had belonged to my grandfather, an open-top, stainless-steel, 50-gallon drum for a fermenting tank, a plastic garbage-can cover drilled with multiple 1" holes for separating the stems from the berries, and an old, heavily-used, wooden basket press I had purchased from an old Italian grower. I used Zinfandel for my homemade wines because the clusters could be plentiful, and fair size in contrast to the second crop Cabernet and Pinot Noir, which had much smaller clusters and were laborious to pick in any substantial quantity. If the weather was favorable after harvest, the quality of a second-crop Zinfandel could be good, and wines made from these grapes, considering the equipment I was using, would be acceptable to drink on a personal basis. You tend to be very forgiving when judging your own house wine. But, to go commercial, in a competitive premium wine marketplace, our wines would have to be of consistently higher quality.

I read, from cover to cover, Amerine and Joslyn's book on the technology and production of wines.[13] I enrolled in a course on the fundamentals of wine chemistry at UC Davis. Davis offered many excellent, short, 1 to 2-day courses conducted by faculty on campus during their vacations and semester breaks. The courses would give a live classroom overview of the subject matter but, more importantly, you returned home with volumes of technical papers and literature pertaining to the subject, which you could further study and review. Over the next 2-3 years, I would take short courses at Davis on the topics of table wine and red wine production, laboratory analysis, and sensory evaluation; from the Wine Lab in Napa, I took a course on wine microbes, problem fermentations, and a study on the contaminate, *Brettanomyces*, which is a wild cellar yeast that can give wine a bad flavor and aroma. I was able to ask questions and discuss technical issues with some of the winemakers who worked at the wineries where we were delivering grapes. I was also able to get technical advice from vendors of winery supplies and equipment. The Cal Poly doctrine of "learning by doing" was also invaluable, because I would benefit from the hands-on experience obtained by doing my own production.

The winter of 1996 had been relatively warm with temperatures in February in the mid-eighties. The weather that followed would not be ideal. Vines started to push early, and three nights of frost in late March burned Chardonnay buds and tender shoots. Light rain in April caused some shatter and poor berry set, and the summer was hot and without the normal morning fog. Harvest came upon us very fast; this enabled us to pick Chardonnay at Dry Creek on August 19, followed by Russian River Pinot Noir on August 29. Overall, the vintage would yield only 149 tons of Pinot Noir, down 22% from the previous year, and our Chardonnay production was off 38%. Grape income fortunately only dropped 13% on account of higher pricing. Future income, coming from the production of our first wine, would add later revenue. But it would be 1998 before we would start to receive any income from wine produced in 1996.

On September 10, 1996, the production of our first estate wine began. I had previously decided I was going to dedicate my first wine to my grandfather Pietro, who as mentioned earlier, was a great influence towards my second career. The question was, what style of wine should this be? Would it be a bold, hearty, dark wine with a strong alcohol content that had the characteristics of his homemade house wine, or something in a milder style? The normal high Brix and alcohol potential from our Dry Creek Zinfandel would support this bold, hearty, alcoholic style; however, Pietro was from Tuscany, which is known for their classic Chianti. Chianti wines are medium bodied, smooth to drink, lower in alcohol, and known for their mixed fruit flavors. For this tribute wine, I would endeavor to make

---

13 *Technology and Production of Table Wines* by M.A. Amerine & M.A. Joslyn, 2nd addition, University of California Press, 1970.

a New-World style Chianti, which would include a traditional small amount of various white grapes, co-fermented with a predominant mix of red grapes. Our Zinfandel and Carignane would replace the traditional red Sangiovese and Canaiolo Nero of Tuscany, and our Golden Chasselas and Burger would be the white grape replacement for the Tuscany Trebbiano and Malvasia grapes. I didn't believe the substitution of our estate grapes in place of the Italian varieties would be of any consequence. I believed co-fermentation of red with white grapes, with the medium body and dominant fruit flavors of the Zinfandel and Carignane would create the equivalent of a Tuscan Chianti. By keeping the content of Zinfandel above 70%, we could label the wine as Zinfandel, and also Estate Grown. I believed this style of wine would have broader appeal to the general marketplace, and so I decided to proceed in this direction.

Batch One: The first batch crushed in our newly constructed winery was 4.49 tons of hand-harvested, 100% head-pruned, old vine, dry-farmed, Dry Creek Zinfandel. The must was evenly distributed among the three open-top fermenters and sulfur dioxide was added to control wild yeasts and bacteria. After a 24-hour ambient soak, the must was inoculated with a cultured, Rhone-isolate, L2226 yeast that was selected for its moderate fermentation rate, enhancement of cherry flavors, low production of hydrogen sulfide, volatile acidity, and resistance to alcohol. Resistance to alcohol was important because alcohol can kill yeast, especially indigenous native yeasts, and you can get a "stuck fermentation" that does not complete to dryness (i.e., the sugar is not completely converted to alcohol). The starting juice tested at 25.0 Brix with 0.560g/100ml total acidity, at a temperature of 78°F.

Jim Forchini punching-down during fermentation, 1996.

Three times a day the ferment of skins and juice was gently punched down using a 12" square stainless flat plate welded on the end of a T-handled long tube. By standing on a 2' × 8' redwood plank placed across the top of the fermenter, the cap of skins that had risen to the surface, buoyed by CO_2 created by the fermentation, were pushed downward into the juice to further extract color and flavor from the grape skins. This Old-World process is called *punch-down*. Larger wineries generally would use a New-World method called *pump-over*, where juice would be pumped from the bottom of the fermenter, and distributed evenly over the top of the must cap by a revolving spray boom or by a hand-held hose. Whether using punch-down or pump-over, the process is called *extraction*. Punch-down is more laborious but a gentler process, which I preferred. It allowed the juice to remain in place undisturbed rather than be pumped through a pump impeller, which I considered harsher on the berries and skins because of impacts, pressure and friction within the pump, hose, nozzle, and spray boom.

After eight days, the fermented juice never exceeded 80°F, and had made a steady progression downward to an intermediate 5.0 Brix at 72°F. The fermenting process was *short vatted,* prior to dryness, to make the fermenters available for a second batch. Four hundred gallons of *free-run* juice (without skins or berries) were drained from the fermenters and pumped to the 3000L stainless tank. The residual must of grape skins and residual liquid was bailed from the fermenters using plastic buckets and placed in the Rossi basket press. It took 2½ baskets, applying 50 psi pressure in the internal water bladder, to extract another 325 gallons of press wine (juice), which was also pumped over to the 3000L tank. The yield of free-run and *press juice* was estimated to be 725 gallons, thus producing 161 gallons/ton. Fermentation in the tank continued at a slow rate and by September 24 sugar had been reduced to 1.2 Brix. On October 3, the juice had dropped in sugar to -0.10 Brix, and the wine was inoculated in the tank with Biotec D *malolactic bacteria* (to kill the yeast), and then pumped to six, 228L, new, medium-toast, American Oak, Radoux barrels, with *toasted heads*, and six, 228L, clean, used, French Oak barrels purchased from another winery. Fifteen additional gallons were stored in a stainless-steel, variable-capacity tank (VCT) to be used for monthly topping off of the barrels (known as replacing the "angels' share"). This routine maintenance was very important to avoid oxidation and the formation of volatile acidity. On October 7, an active *ML (malolactic) fermentation* in the barrels was actively proceeding, as evidenced by the solid barrel *bungs* popping out. Breathable silicone bungs, that allowed the CO_2 from secondary fermentation to escape, were put in place. On November 18, 1996, and again on February 12, 1997, the wine was pumped from the 12 barrels to the 3000L stainless tank and SO_2 was adjusted to maintain control of the micro-organisms and absorbed oxygen head. The barrels were cleaned from residue by inserting a rotating sprinkler in the *bung hole* of an upside-down supported barrel and rinsing with water until the water ran clear. The process of pumping the wine from barrels to tank, and returning the wine back to clean barrels, was called *racking* and was used to clarify the wine and remove precipitated solids from the interior of the barrel.

Batch 2: On September 25 and 26, a second batch of 4.2 tons was harvested, consisting of 83% Zinfandel, 7% Carignane, and 10% mixed white varietals. The combined lot was crushed and distributed to two fermenters. A juice sample tested 23.8 Brix with 0.633 total acidity at 69°F. The lower sugar and higher acid content of this batch were because this batch used second-crop Zinfandel and Carignane. This was very much desired as it would provide balance once mixed with the higher Brix and lower acid wine produced from the first batch. On September 27, the juice was inoculated with the same L2226 yeast. Fermentation commenced, and by October 4, the sugar had dropped to 0.5 Brix. The wine was pressed on October 4, and transferred to the 3,000L tank. The yield was again estimated to be about 725 gallons. By October 7, the wine was -1.2 Brix, and no detectable sugar was measured, meaning the wine was totally dry. After inoculating in the tank with ML bacteria, the wine was pumped to 12 228L, used French Oak barrels, and 15 gallons were added to the VCT for topping. On November 21, 1996, and March 2, 1997, this wine was racked and laid to rest in barrels along with the first batch.

At this point, our inventory of wine was 1,440 gallons in French Oak barrels, of which 25% was new oak, and 30 gallons stored in the stainless VCT for topping. In 1997, we were going to need additional equipment for the final processing of the 1996 wine. Orders were placed for a Marchesio 5000L stainless tank, a GAI 500 monobloc bottling machine, a Della Toffolla 40cm, 19-plate filter, and a Gluefast labeler. This equipment came at great expense. We were counting on that expense being offset by the increase in net income from eventual wine sales compared to the income had we only sold the 8.69 tons of grapes to another winery.

On June 1, 1997, the combined composition of Batch 1 and Batch 2 was 92% Zinfandel, 5% mixed white, and 3% Carignane. Bench trials were performed, and it was decided to blend all 12 barrels from Batch 1 with five barrels from Batch 2. The composition now became 95% Zinfandel, 3% white and 2% Carignane, which gave the wine a little more body and color. These 17 barrels were pumped into the new 5000L tank for blending, and the remaining seven Batch 2 barrels were kept for bulk sale or future blending. By August 8, 1997, the blended wine in the 5000L tank was well developed, had a nice aroma on the nose, a taste of bright, crisp, fruit flavors, and was medium body in structure. After doing some *sensory evaluation*, a noted slight sharpness on the finish was softened by reducing the total acidity from 0.640 to 0.610g/100ml, using potassium carbonate. This adjustment provided a smoother finish on the palatte with better balance and mouthfeel.

On December 23, the wine was rough-filtered using Seitz 7-micron filter pads, and by January 29, 1998, we were ready to bottle. The wine was polished-filtered to 3 microns, and with a rented *sparging* machine, the bottles were purged of oxygen with nitrogen gas, gravity filled, and vacuum corked using the GAI monoblock. Five men packaged 426 cases of wine, consisting of 12 750ml bottles per case, at a rate of 50 cases an hour. A factory representative from GAI, the provider of the bottling machine, helped on this initial bottling, assisted by me, sons Michael and Andrew, and a friend who was a knowledgeable cellar master. We all had a good time.

The bottling went well, and the unlabeled wine was laid to rest horizontally in bins for bottle aging and future labelling.

The back label would read:

This wine is dedicated to my maternal grandfather, Pietro Bernacchi, who was called Papa by his children and Nonno by his grandchildren. He came to America in 1908 from Tuscany, Italy. Although he worked in the oil fields by day, his true love was farming and his agrarian skills were reflected in his magnificent small farm where he produced fruits, vegetables and a wine he called Zinfandella. This fruity Tuscan style blend is similar to the type he would make for family, however it is softer with more suppleness and less astringency. Tanti Grazie Nonno for your inspiration.

For the front label we used a Caravaggio Baccho, circa 1556, taken from a poster Anita and I had purchased at the Uffizi Galleria in Florence, Italy. We had a graphic artist center the print in an arched window and bordered it to connect with an enlarged Roman styled font under the F and I of the Forchini Header. Was this legal? We weren't exactly sure, but decided on our next trip to Italy, we would visit the Uffizi and find out.

CHAPTER 8

Epilogue

THE FIRST VINTAGE FROM Forchini Vineyards & Winery in 1996 marked the beginning of a 24-year period, during which Jim and Anita operated the vineyard and winery enterprise they had built over the preceding 30 years. When Jim embarked on writing his story in 2020, no doubt he had in mind providing his readers with recollections of the entire period. But he ran out of time with his unanticipated and sudden death in January 2022. That left it to others to continue his story beyond that production of his 1996 tribute wine, *Papa Nonno*, the first release from the new Forchini winery.

Jim's story would be incomplete without a closing part. In the preceding chapters, he has told his story through 1996, and in his own personal style of storytelling. The last years have been left for his family and friends to write. However, what is said about those final years must not take liberties with Jim's original intention: To tell **his story** in **his own way**. Therefore, this epilogue is confined to a summary of what happened in those years, without the colorful detail that only Jim Forchini could have provided. What follows in no way attempts to mimic his unusual style of writing. Its only purpose is to conclude the story of Jim and Anita Forchini.

Vineyards

Jim Forchini remained firmly in control of his vineyards as the next 24 years began. His rigorous diligence never faltered, as shown in his continuous improvement of both the Dry Creek and Old Redwood Highway ranches. He remained totally invested in his vineyards, financially and emotionally. They reflected his complete involvement in their development and well-being.

Andrew Forchini at right with son Donovan (age 7) during 2020 harvest.

But Jim did not work alone. Andrew, the youngest son, began working in the vineyards immediately after graduating from viticulture school in 1998, becoming the Forchini vineyard manager a year later. Andrew was groomed by Jim, and Jim's mentoring clearly influenced Andrew's sense of responsibility for the vineyards in his charge. Jim and Andrew shared similar outlooks on vineyard management and environmental stewardship, and they worked effectively with one another. To the casual observer, Forchini vineyards under their care seemed more carefully constructed and better managed than nearby vineyards of many other winegrowers. With only a few exceptions, Forchini vineyards were a cut above the others.

View of Dry Creek Cabernet Sauvignon vineyard as seen from winery looking west, 2010.

For years, when driving up the entranceway to the winery from Dry Creek Road, one could see flocks of sheep grazing on the cover crop amidst the vine rows. The sheep were effective in keeping the cover crop under control, no doubt improving the effectiveness of the irrigation program, but also helping to maintain the attractive appearance of the vineyard blocks. Few vineyards were maintained in this manner, but Forchini vineyards were.

The vineyard workforce was stable and committed to the long term. The workers were well cared for, and they stayed with the Forchinis for many years. Such workforce loyalty reflected Jim and Anita's sense of responsibility for their employees. Jim had learned this from his grandparents and parents during his boyhood. For Anita, such caring simply flowed from her caring personality.

Much of the Forchini grape production was processed as estate wines at the winery, but as in former years, a considerable tonnage of fruit was sold to other wineries. The quality of Forchini grapes was dependably high, and this expanded the number of wineries buying Forchini fruit. Finding homes for harvested grapes was never a problem.[14]

---

14 Jim Forchini was particular about the buyers of his fruit; he wasn't interested in selling to just anyone. One such buyer in the 1990s was Mick Schroeter, then the winemaker at Geyser Peak Winery. Mick related to the editor a story about being "interviewed" by Jim Forchini on Mick's application to purchase Forchini fruit. It was as if Mick was applying for a job. It was an extraordinary, and amusing, experience for Mick.

Night harvesting Pinot Noir, 2020.

Sheep crazing in vineyard, helping control cover crop.

The vagaries of weather, common to the early years of Forchini grape growing, remained as daunting as ever during the years following the initial winemaking. Jim coped with whatever nature threw his way. He had no choice but to find ways to survive the drought that might develop in any year, endure heavy rains that could arrive in other years, survive untimely and devastatingly high temperatures that could destroy grapes ready for harvest, or get through times of devastating frost or pestilence. He paid close attention to what could happen, and he did what he could to avoid damage to his crops and to his vineyards. He continued to participate in industry associations, where knowledge shared with other winegrowers sometimes provided salvation for a winegrower faced with possible devastation.

Harvests, while busy and often hectic, were managed with order and confidence. Picking at night, when the temperatures were much lower than during the day, was common practice for most winegrowers, including the Forchinis. The harvest crew, supplemented by seasonal workers, always included family members in addition to Andrew, the vineyard manager. Jim was usually in the seat of a tractor or a truck, and Mike and sometimes several of the grandchildren were busy with other tasks in the field. Anita and Carla contributed their talents on the administrative side back at the winery, where grape deliveries were processed. It was very much a family affair.

Forchini family at Dry Creek Ranch, 1999. (L–R) Mike, Carla, Andrew, Anita, and Jim.

For several harvests after 2017, the cabernet sauvignon was mechanically harvested. A selective mechanical harvesting machine was hired: an Optimum 890 Selectiv' Process 2, de-stemming and sorting machine made by Pellenc, a French company specializing in viticulture. The machine straddled each vine row, and stripped berries from clusters and sorted out material other than grape (so-called MOG). The picked berries were dumped into gondolas that were towed alongside the harvester as the harvester moved down vine rows. The objective of the mechanical harvesting was to more rapidly deliver freshly picked and de-stemmed fruit to the winery for immediate crushing and fermentation. Labor savings and the higher quality of freshly delivered grapes justified the cost of hiring the harvester. Use of selective mechanical harvesting, while not novel in American viniculture, was an aggressive step toward using newer technology for a small winery like Forchini.

Optimum 890 mechanical harvester by Pellenc used for harvesting Cabernet Sauvignon, 2017.

Canopy management was greatly facilitated by a mechanical trimming rig. Jim had first fabricated such a tractor-mounted machine in the 1990s, and it was replaced with a larger version of the same kind in later years. The rig shown here was just one example of how Jim managed his vineyards.

Cane trimming rig operated by Andrew Forchini.

Forchini vineyards grew mostly Zinfandel, Pinot Noir, and Cabernet Sauvignon, but also had substantial acreage in Carignane, Chardonnay, Chasselas, with a few other varieties in lesser quantities. These were the *varieties* Jim had cultivated in earlier years, and he continued to grow what had been successful in the past and what currently commanded good prices in the marketplace for grapes. As in the earlier years, he did not hesitate to tear out vines that were no longer productive, or varieties of grapes no longer commanding prices competitive with other grape varieties.

Production

Following his initial 1996 tribute release (Papa Nonno, the Tuscan blend resembling a chianti), Jim made five additional wines at the winery. The wines produced by Forchini Winery were made entirely from estate grapes. Only four of the six wines produced (listed in the table on the following page) were named *varietals* (including the Paradiso); the other two wines were blends based on Zinfandel (Papa Nonno) or Cabernet Sauvignon (Beau Sierra). While all the wines were Italian-style, all fruit was estate grown, and with no Italian *varieties*. Released first in 2004, the Paradiso (rosé of Cabernet Sauvignon) was discontinued after only a few years. Chardonnay was removed from the ORH ranch after the 2011 harvest and was replanted with Pinot Noir.

	Vintage	Style
Papa Nonno	1996	Tuscan-style blend of Zinfandel with white varieties, resembling a Chianti
Cabernet Sauvignon	1996	Cabernet Sauvignon with minor Carignane blending
Old Vine Zinfandel	1996	90-year-old Zinfandel vines, robust red wine
Chardonnay	2002	Oak barrel aged, a light and crisp wine
Beau Sierra	2003	Bordeaux-style red blend of Cabernet Sauvignon with minor red grape blending components
Paradiso	2004	Rosé of Cabernet Sauvignon

Paradiso, Rosé of Cabernet Sauvignon.

Three thousand cases of wine were processed annually at the winery as estate wine. In addition, large volumes of wine were produced and sold regularly to buyers as bulk wine for their own bottled wine programs. Bulk wine sales plus unprocessed grapes annually accounted for about three-quarters of the total harvested grapes; the other quarter of the fruit, selected for highest quality, went into the making of the estate wines.

Sierra (at left) during Pinot Noir harvest, 2014.

Jim remained the winemaker. Carla's daughter, Sierra, studied enology at UC Davis, graduating in 2013. She came to work with her grandfather for the harvest in 2014. She was understudy to Jim, working at the winery for a while until she decided to spread her wings, and move on. She travelled to Australia in late 2014 where she worked harvests in Western Australia, Victoria; and even worked a harvest in New Zealand, before settling in Tasmania in 2017. She remained in Tasmania as winemaker for a noted winery, and it became apparent that she had no intention of returning to California. This left Jim with no heir-apparent—at least in terms of a winemaker. This must have disappointed him, because he was then without someone to share and eventually relieve him of some the growing workload on the winemaking side of the business.

Marketing

Anita attending to wine club matters, 2006.

Monetization of wines depended on an aggressive marketing program. The Forchinis established a members-only wine club, which was largely organized by Carla, hence its name "Carla's Club." A tasting room was incorporated into the design of a third new building, which was situated on the downhill side of the winery building. This new building housed a tasting room, offices, a kitchen, dining room, and a small warehouse, all on the ground floor. The second story of the building was a residential apartment intended for rental.

Paolo (age 10) in foreground and Beau (age 12) at the bottle-capping station, 2017.

Anita administered the wine club from her office in the tasting room building. She dealt with club members and managed the public affairs program. An assistant was engaged to operate the tasting room. Jim maintained a desk in the same office alongside Anita, attending to warehousing, distribution, and sales issues. Mike focused on marketing, particularly dealing with distributors, and he pitched in during harvests and for special winery events. Andrew was always busy in the vineyards or at the winery. Sierra stayed in the winery for the most part (she admitted to not enjoying the public nature of the tasting room). Even the younger grandchildren pitched in during busy times. The entire operation was certainly a family affair.

The public face of Forchini Vineyards & Winery was advanced through numerous media avenues. The masthead of the winery was prominent in all correspondence and advertisements. Based on the image of the original Papa Nonno label, the winery was immediately recognized by the familiar image of the young Bacchus, as represented in the Caravaggio painting:

Forchini masthead, featuring the young Bacchus depicted in oil painting
by Caravaggio (1556), Uffizi Galleria, Florence.

Promotion of the Sonoma County wine industry relied in large measure on the wine events held each year (Winter Wineland, Barrel Tasting, Taste of Sonoma, etc.), and on the private events staged by the individual wineries. The Forchinis participated in most of the industry-wide events, and they hosted numerous private events for wine club members. While the expenses associated with these promotional efforts were not trivial, the benefits of participation were judged to outweigh the associated costs. It was all essential to advancing the Forchini image in the marketplace.

Zinfandel award for best in class, best in region, California State Fair, 1999.
(L-R) Carla, Andrew, Mike, Jim, and Anita Forchini.

Annual wine competitions pitted wineries against one another, providing opportunities for each participating winery to showcase their wines before discerning judges. From the very first vintage of Zinfandel in 1996, Forchini Zinfandel was annually awarded prizes for excellence in one competition or another. Cabernet Sauvignon and Pinot Noir vintages from 1998 won honors, and both received awards every year thereafter. Papa Nonno began winning honors in 2002. It remained a top competitor through to the last vintage in 2016, after which all red wine vintages were sold as bulk wine (see section on "Winding Down" below). The last vintage from the winery was the 2017 Chardonnay, which was rated as "exceptional" in the 2018 World Wine Championships. Any wines that received awards earned the winery bragging rights. Jim proudly displayed the accolades his wines had won, and he rarely missed an opportunity to remind visiting members of the public about the honors he had garnered.

Jim, Anita, and Carla Forchini on Anita's birthday,
Agave Restaurant, Healdsburg, December 2017.

Nearly every winery maintains a website providing the visiting public information about the winery, the wines, and the people running the place. The websites also contain information about winery events, all in the interest of advertising the greater benefits available to wine club members at the winery. The Forchinis devoted special attention to this channel for public outreach. Anita and Carla were prime movers in the push for an active website. Carla took a leave of absence from her teaching job to devote full-time attention to the administrative side of the business, incorporating numerous improvements, including bringing the winery website up to industry standards.

View from Tasting Room patio looking west across Dry Creek Valley, 2015

Tasting rooms at some wineries are excellent, others not so good. Forchini's tasting room was small but very pleasant. A person was on staff to serve as the wine pourer in the tasting room, although either Jim, Anita, or other family members would serve in the tasting room when needed. Based on comments from visitors to the tasting room, as seen on industry websites carrying information about area wineries, their experiences were usually positive. Most comments sang high praises for the hospitality they enjoyed during their visits; hardly ever was there a negative comment posted by some disgruntled visitor.

Anita and Carla serving at Wine & Food Affair event, 2006.

The outside patio was an inviting place to sit and enjoy the ambience of the Dry Creek Valley off to the west. Some visitors stayed for many hours; some visitors enjoyed their picnic lunches in the comfort of the patio. Some visitors just stayed a while; time enough to taste some wine, perhaps purchase some favorite bottle, or enjoy a cheerful conversation with whoever was pouring in the tasting room. Repeat visitors were common. Customer satisfaction was obviously a top priority.

Special events usually drew small groups of people. The spreads were never lavish; foods offered tended to be modest comfort foods, in the Italian manner. The foods were designed to pair with the offered wines. Events were simple, lacking much of the frivolity found in many other wineries. But the experience was always rewarding, and very much appreciated by the visitors. They tended to return.

Trajectory of Wine Industry

Over the past several decades, the Sonoma County wine industry has raised the priority of promotion through aggressive marketing. For the individual winery, this has translated to increasing pressure to participate in wine industry activities and to host private events. Wine clubs have become major business activities for many wineries as a vehicle for introducing members to new wine releases, and providing available wines for purchase, usually at preferred prices. Wine clubs are all about promotion and generating sales. Most wine clubs generate reliable income streams from wines sold to the members. In fact, for some wineries, wine clubs are their exclusive outlets for public sales. The real cost of the wine clubs is not only the cost of the events, but the burden wine club operation places on winery management. This was especially troublesome for a small winery like Forchini.

Not all proprietors appreciated this reality. While most understood the importance of such promotion, not all fully understood the adverse financial impact, or the dedication required of winery management. Moreover, as Sonoma County wineries became more broadly known and developed larger followings, the numbers of visitors to regions like Dry Creek swelled. Some of the visitors were not the best-behaved; some were outright undesirable. Some proprietors simply declined to participate in industry promotional activities; some scaled back their hospitality programs.

As the popularity of Forchini wines increased, and more people discovered the attraction of visiting the Forchini winery, Jim was becoming less enamored with the hospitality side of the business. Anita never would say anything; she was far too reserved and polite to reveal her honest feelings in this regard. But Jim would speak out, and he made it very clear to his friends that he was losing interest in running an entertainment business. He would lament that he was a winegrower first, a winemaker second; all the rest was not for him. Such sentiments were expressed by Jim as early as 2018, suggesting something was going to change. It was just a matter of time.

In addition to the nuisance of the hospitality business (as Jim was increasingly characterizing it), the burden of increased regulation was becoming oppressive. At the local, county, and state levels, new rules increasingly constrained the ways in which proprietors could run their businesses. While many of the regulations served noble purposes, particularly those in the interest of environmental protection, some rules did not seem justified. Jim would comply with the rules, but that didn't mean he always liked them. He would act responsibly and follow the law where it was clear, but he'd let you know how he felt about something he did not respect. To many of his friends, it was clear that the regulatory regime was wearing him down, and that his patience was being stretched thin.

Winding Down

During most winters after the year 2000, Jim and Anita would travel to Europe after the harvest and crush. With the new vintages in barrels, they would leave Sonoma and travel for several weeks, perhaps a month, to some place in Europe (the Adriatic, Italy, Portugal, France, Switzerland, Germany, Sweden, Ireland, and the British Isles, to name a few). They loved these times and talked endlessly about their adventures with friends when they had returned home. However, by 2018 Anita realized she could no longer keep up with the pace set by Jim, nor could she handle the stress presented by many of the routine difficulties any traveler would experience. She was becoming tired. Jim recognized this, and their traveling days soon came to an end.

On the business side, it was also becoming clear that Anita would no longer be able to manage her business role as in the past, and this meant some major changes in winery management were going to be needed. The children were now grown and pursuing their own lives: Mike was running his own business in Arcata; Carla was a totally involved school teacher in Healdsburg; and Andrew, while remaining the Forchini vineyard manager, did not seem especially interested in the customer and marketing side of the business. Sierra, the promising winemaker, remained in Australia with little immediate prospect of returning to California. Jim needed to consider how these new realities, in addition to his own growing attitudes toward the business, would affect the way forward. By 2019, Jim decided to cease wine production and liquidate the wine inventory. This meant a gradual termination of the marketing program: no more participation in future industry events, no further special events, no more acceptance of new wine club memberships. The business would be reduced and return primarily to winegrowing. When grapes could not be sold to other wineries, Forchini would continue to produce wine for bulk sale. These two business streams would be sufficient to support Jim and Anita for a long while.

The last bottled vintages of all Forchini wines, except Chardonnay, were in 2016; Chardonnay was discontinued with the 2017 vintage. The last sale from the tasting room was October 10, 2020, by which time the entire inventory of wines had been sold from the warehouse. What remained were the sale of grapes and production of a limited volume of bulk wine.

Anita and Jim in Sausalito, March 2021, three weeks before Anita passed away.

By Christmas 2020, Anita had progressively weakened, and she was becoming infirm. In early March 2021, she suffered a brain hemorrhage. She was released from the Santa Rosa hospital to return home, but on March 17, she suffered a second stroke, which put her back in the hospital in Santa Rosa. She remained there and gradually declined over the following week. On the afternoon of March 23, 2021, she passed away with family at her side.

Jim was grief-stricken and understandably lost. He had shut down their winery and pared back the business to a shadow of its former stature. And now he has lost his wife of nearly 60 years and his closest friend. It was a terrible time for him.

Jim and Carla Forchini, Half Moon Bay, December 2021.

Jim spent time with his family and friends in the months following. Just before Christmas 2021, he was in Half Moon Bay with Carla having lunch with his younger brother, Pete. They wandered down to Miramar Beach where the famed Mavericks surfing competition is held, enjoying the seaside air. Jim had his dog with him, who decided to chase after something interesting. Jim ran after the pup, but about an hour later, Jim suffered a stroke. This landed him in the hospital where he spent the night under observation. The attending doctor advised Carla that this was but a warning of what might come for Jim.

After the Christmas holidays in 2021, Jim was fishing for crab on the Sonoma coast accompanied by his dog. The dog again chased after something, and Jim went in pursuit. He was struck by a heart attack and died on the spot. That was January 21, 2022, just nine months after Anita had passed.

Now Jim would be reunited with Anita.

Preserving the Family Legacy

No one anticipated that Jim would die so suddenly. Despite the December episode, he seemed in robust health. He was learning to cope with his grief, and his outlook was positive. His death truly came as a shock for his family and his many friends.

Mike and Andrew Forchini, Dry Creek Ranch, February 2022.

Jim had intended that his ranches be evenly shared with the three siblings, Mike, Carla, and Andrew. But he left no instructions on how the sharing should be accomplished. His wishes seem to have been characteristically tacit. For years he had conducted himself in the winegrowing business in this informal manner, and, notwithstanding some disappointments, his business methods had served him well. He must have assumed that the three siblings would sort things out, and do so amicably.

This was not to be. For reasons that need not be addressed in this book, the three siblings concluded that the ranches should be divided. Mike and Carla became co-proprietors of the Dry Creek ranch, which included the vineyards, the winery with its tasting room and barn/shop, and the residence; Andrew became sole owner of the Old Redwood Highway ranch. This reallocation of the properties was finalized in April 2023.

As of this writing, it is unclear how each new proprietor would operate their respective properties, or to what extent they would cooperate with one another.

It's also not clear that Jim or Anita had any preconceptions about their legacy. They didn't leave any indication of how they wanted what they had built over the years to be carried forward. They appear to have presumed that Mike, Carla, and Andrew would figure it out, the way they had always done.

In the introductory chapter of this book, Jim emphasizes his hope that the story he is telling will be of inspiration to others. He offers his advice:

> *Don't be afraid to follow a dream, be willing to take uncertain risks, and trust your instincts if you believe in yourself. Time is precious and should not be wasted because it can never be replaced. Don't look back and regret what you should or could have done. If you move forward with caution, do your homework, study the facts, and evaluate the variables before making major decisions, you will be off to a good start.*

Jim certainly followed his dreams. He seemed aware of the risks he was taking, and he came to grips with their implications. After careful evaluation and soul-searching, he was not in the least hesitant to make up his mind and choose the path he would take. It's not apparent he ever looked back, or harbored regrets for something he should have done differently. Yet, he learned from his mistakes and avoided repeating things that had gone poorly for him in the past. He applied himself carefully to the problem at hand, relying on the methodical and analytical skills that he had acquired as a highly trained professional engineer. He summoned the skills he had learned during his long and active life, from his childhood in the Central Valley of California, to his successful mechanical engineering profession, and eventually to include those of his chosen profession as a winegrower. He had no problem designing and building his winery. For many smaller but equally important projects, such as designing and fabricating some new mechanical device, he was entirely comfortable. He was self-reliant, yet never bashful about asking for advice. An intensely proud man, he was not always happy to be given advice, but he knew humility, and was not one to summarily discard an idea simply because it wasn't his own. He listened carefully and evaluated what he was told, and if thought to be a better way of doing something, he accepted it as what he had to do. In the end, he relied on his own mind, and he trusted his instincts.

Jim pursued all of this with careful consideration for Anita and his family. He was faithful to his commitment as a husband, father, and head of his family. He was totally committed to their welfare. He always ensured they were every bit as involved as he was.

To quote his eldest son, Michael:

> *Dad was the most successful, smartest, and hard-headed man I knew. My respect for both him and Mom are very strong. I am thankful and grateful for their hard work, accomplishments, and legacy.*

> *Michael Forchini*
> *July 7, 2023*

Jim Forchini at 2015 Solstice Dinner, Dry Creek.

Glossary

THE GLOSSARY IN THE FOLLOWING PAGES contains terms as they appear in the preceding text. Most of the terms are common to the wine industry in California. Where a word appears in a definition in italics, the italicized word is defined elsewhere in the Glossary.[15]

Term	Meaning
ambient soak	After crushed grapes are placed in a fermentation tank, the *must* is allowed to soak at ambient pressure for some period of time, the purpose being to allow the liquid to gain some of the color and flavors from the crushed grape skins.
AVA	Acronym for American Viticultural Area, defined as a delimited grape growing region defined by geographical features, the boundaries of which have been recognized and defined.
AXR	A *rootstock* developed in California that is especially resistant to *phylloxera*, the disease that afflicts grape vines. By 1980 nearly two-thirds of Napa and Sonoma vineyards were planted with this rootstock.

---

15 Three sources provide useful definitions of terms: (1) Several of the terms are described within the chapters written by Jim Forchini; (2) many other terms are defined in Karen MacNeil, *The Wine Bible* (New York: Workman Publishing, 2001); (3) a third source is word search on the internet via Google.

Brettanomyces	Also called "Brett," Brettanomyces is a type of yeast commonly found in wines, which can cause significant spoilage through the production of phenol compounds.
Brix	A measure of dissolved solids in a liquid; in grape growing, refers to the level of sugar in juice; expressed in degrees as measured by a *hydrometer* or *refractometer*. One degree of Brix is equal to 1 gram of sucrose per 100 grams of solution.
budding	A cutting from a healthy vine is *grafted* to another vine, usually a *rootstock*, by inserting the cutting into a cut (notch) and securing it to the rootstock. The grafting process is known as "budding."
bulk wine	Wine not in a bottle; bought and sold by wineries of all tiers, for various purposes.
bung	Made commonly of wood or plastic, a bung is used as a stopper in a barrel with a *bung hole*. Modern bungs are designed to allow gasses within the barrel to escape, but not allow ambient gasses to enter the barrel. The bung functions like a cork (stopper) in a wine bottle.
bung hole	A hole bored in the side of a wine barrel through which wine is pumped into, or drawn out of, the barrel. A *bung* is inserted into the bung hole to seal the barrel.
Burger grape	Burger is a white wine grape of French origin, also known by its French name, *Monbadon*; formerly in common use in California, but now used primarily in bulk jug wine production.
carbonic maceration	A type of *fermentation* in which bunches of uncrushed grapes are placed whole inside a closed tank; the weight of the grapes crushes the grapes at the tank bottom, while the grapes in the upper levels remain intact. The juices released from the crushed grapes at the tank bottom ferment in the usual manner. Fermentation takes place within the uncrushed grapes in the upper level of the tank, resulting in a juicier style of wine.

CAWG	Acronym for California Association of Winegrape Growers, a state-wide organization, whose purpose is to protect and promote the interests of California wine grape growers by providing members a unified voice, effective advocacy, and strong leadership.
Chasselas	A wine grape variety that can make a full, dry, and fruity white wine; also suitable as a table grape and as a blending *variety*.
CNCGGA	Acronym meaning California North Coast Grape Growers Association, which, for nearly 40 years (1960-1999), represented the interests of California North Coast grape growers on matters of production forecasting, pricing, and industry issues such as labor regulations.
CO$_2$	Carbon dioxide, a gaseous compound released during *fermentation* and barrel-aging of grapes. In some places, it is written CO2.
contadina	An Italian word meaning peasant woman; the masculine form of the word is *contadino*. As used here, this refers to peasant farmworkers working in the fields in Italy.
cordon	Synonymous with cane, a wooded *shoot* stemming from a grape vine's vertical stalk, bent to extend the growing vine wood horizontally from which grape buds and other shoots grow; usually supported by a *trellis* wire. Some refer to cordons as the vine's arms.
cordon pruning	A method of pruning grape vines in which the positions of the *cordons* are established by the training process; all fruiting and renewal spurs sprout from this area. Sometimes called *spur pruning*.
cross cultivation	The tillage of a vineyard, field, or orchard in which the cultivation is in one direction followed by cultivation at right angles to the first; done to achieve more complete tillage of the field. Also called "cross ploughing."
DC	An acronym referring to "Dry Creek Ranch." Located at 5143 Dry Creek Road, Healdsburg. DC was the second Forchini home ranch.

disc harrow	A tractor-drawn farm implement (a harrow) comprising usually two rows of sharp circular discs, often deeply serrated, separated along the axles by several inches. The axles are hinged at mid-span and are connected, one forward of the other; the hinge angle is adjusted by a rack-and-cawl device that allows the operator to move the axles into "V" configurations so that the discs can cut into the soil and turn over the cut material they form.
dry/dryness	Describes any wine that doesn't contain significant amounts of residual grape sugar following fermentation.
dusting	Blowing air mixed with dry insecticide and/or fungicide directly onto a grape vine for the purpose of controlling insects and/or mildew. Dusting is a routine vineyard maintenance activity.
El Niño	A 2-7-year cyclic climate pattern where, around the end of the calendar year, warmer water concentrates in the eastern Pacific Ocean along the equator in response to weakening westerly trade winds, causing higher pressure to build along the coast of South America. A strong Pacific jet stream is drawn to the south, resulting in a northward deflection of major winter storms, usually into the northwest of the United States, which can be a major factor in deepening droughts in California. At times, however, this stream can guide repeated atmospheric rivers along its southern edge, resulting in northern California flooding. The opposing pattern to El Niño is La Niña, where colder than usual water temperatures are found in the Central and Eastern Pacific Ocean due to deep upwelling as the warmer surface waters are pushed west by stronger than usual trade winds. El Niño is characterized by high-pressure systems over the Western Pacific and low pressure over the Eastern Pacific, while La Niña is characterized by low pressure over the Western Pacific and high-pressure systems over the Eastern Pacific. This allows a weaker and more variable jet stream to swing to the north. In La Niña years, California tends to experience more irregular rainfall, but can, in some years, experience heavier storms relieving local droughts.
enology	The science that deals with wine and winemaking.

extraction	During *fermentation*, a cap of grape skins rises to the top of the *fermenter*, buoyed by escaping CO_2. To extract more color and flavor from the skins by maintaining contact of the skins and juice, either the cap can be gently *punched down* toward the bottom of the *fermenter*, or juice can be pumped from the bottom of the *fermenter* and sprayed over the cap (*pump over*). Either process is called "extraction."
farm	In Central and much of Northern California, agricultural properties are called farms as opposed to *ranches*, which is what Sonoma County agricultural properties are commonly called.
fermentation	Chemical process wherein sugar in grape juice is converted to alcohol; it occurs naturally on account of the native yeasts on the skins of the grapes, but is often enhanced by added yeasts with desired properties; called *primary fermentation*.
fermenter	A vessel into which crushed grapes (juice and skins) are pumped and where natural *primary fermentation* occurs.
free run	At the end of both *primary fermentation* and *carbonic maceration*, the wine is usually drained off the skins, which have not been subjected to any mechanical crushing pressure. This wine is known as "free run."
gondola	A bin for transporting picked grapes, usually large and mounted on the bed of a truck or a wagon, and often gimballed such that the bin can be tipped so that the grape contents can spill into some other vessel, for instance, a conveyor hopper.
graft	The process of attaching a *stem* or bud of one vine to the trunk or *rootstock* of another vine; virtually all wine grape *varieties* are grafted onto disease-resistant *rootstocks*.
Head-pruning (pollard)	A type of vine training in which only a few shoots are allowed to develop at the head (top) on the vine stalk; all buds grow from these few shoots which develop to canes (branches). Eventually, such pruning leads to stout vine stalks that can withstand the weight of fruit without *trellising*. This pruning style, also called pollard pruning, is common to Zinfandel. The old vine Zinfandel vines common to the Forchini vineyards are the result.

hydrometer	In a graduated tube, a liquid's dissolved sugar is measured by the specific gravity of the liquid; based on data tables, the specific gravity is correlated to *Brix*.
Johnnie Popper	The nickname awarded to the John Deere Model M tractors that were used in many Sonoma County vineyards. They were commonly referred to by the local growers as "Johnnie Poppers." This was because the low-speed, high-torque, 2-cylinder engine had a huge fly wheel to maintain inertia, and the result was a pop-pop-pop sound as the large pistons cycled through four strokes of internal combustion.
malolactic bacteria	The benign bacteria that cause *malolactic (ML) fermentation;* often introduced by inoculation after primary fermentation is completed, in part to avoid unpleasant strains of bacteria from spoiling the wine.
ML fermentation	Refers to malolactic fermentation, in which tart malic acid (imagine the tartness of apple) is converted to softer lactic acid (imagine the acid in milk). ML fermentation takes place during barrel aging and is caused by benign bacteria reacting with residual wine acids. It has nothing to do with *primary fermentation*, in which sugar is converted to alcohol. It is often referred to as *secondary fermentation*.
mold board plow	A plow design including a wooden shoulder with optimized shape for efficient lifting up and turning over of soil or sod cut by an iron blade while pulled through the soil with a minimal expenditure of force.
must	The juice and liquid pulp, plus skins, stems, and seeds produced by initial crushing or pressing of grapes before *fermentation*.
native yeast	In the absence of oxygen, yeast converts the sugars of the fruit into alcohol and carbon dioxide through the process of *fermentation*. Native yeast occurs naturally on grapes, and presence of yeast is crucial for fermentation of the grape juice from crushed (pressed) grapes.

non-trellis planting	Some *varieties*, such as old vine Zinfandel, typically have stout vine trunks that are sufficient to keep the entire vine upright off the ground. These vines are *head-pruned*. No *trellis* system is required, which allows cultivation and other vineyard management work to be done easily around the vines. *Trellised planting* involves a trellis system of posts strung with wires to support the vines, creating corridors between rows of vines. This kind of trellis system is more restrictive for vineyard management.
notch-graft	A method of *grafting* vines wherein a V-shaped notch is cut in a vine trunk into which a new bud is to be grafted; the bud is cut so that it fits snugly into this notch. The assembly of bud and trunk is wrapped and covered for protection from weather and insects.
ORH	An acronym referring the "Old Redwood Highway Ranch." ORH was the first Forchini home ranch. Located at 12320 Old Redwood Highway south of Healdsburg, California.
phylloxera	A highly destructive small aphid that attacks the vine's roots and destroys the vine by preventing the roots from absorbing water; the only solution is to replant the affected vines with native American *rootstocks*, which are resistant to the disease, and then *graft* wine grape vines to the new rootstock.
pollard pruning	Refers to cutting a tree or vine back to the main trunk to promote the growth of a dense head of foliage atop a free-standing trunk. Pollard pruning is a common method of pruning for old vine Zinfandel vines.
press wine	After *fermentation,* when the liquid is drained from the *fermenter,* the *must* is gently pressed to remove more liquid. The liquid is called "press wine."
primary fermentation	A process whereby the sugar in juice from crushed or pressed grapes is converted to alcohol in the presence of *native yeasts.*
prune head	Refers to pruning a *pollard* vine, such as old vine Zinfandel.

pump over	An *extraction* process in which juice is pumped from the bottom of the *fermenter* and sprayed over the cap of grape skins, seeds, and stems (the *must*) that has risen to the top of the *fermenter*.
punch down	An *extraction* process where the cap of grape skins, seeds, and stems that has risen to the top of the *fermenter* (the *must*) is gently pushed down toward the bottom of the fermenter.
racking	The process of allowing solids to settle to the bottom of a vat or barrel, then pouring or drawing off the clear wine; repeated racking is often necessary to remove precipitates that form during the aging process.
ranch	In Sonoma County agricultural properties are called *ranches* instead of *farms*. Most agricultural properties in the San Joaquin and Sacramento valleys are called farms. On a Sonoma County ranch, it makes no difference whether you are raising cattle, chickens, growing prunes, hops, apples, or grapes.
refractometer	An instrument that measures the dissolved sugar in a liquid by the change in the liquid's key optical properties, namely, the extent to which the dissolved sugar bends the plane of polarized light; the refractive index and the polarization (the extent to which the dissolved sugar in the liquid had rotated the plane of polarized light); these properties have been calibrated to measure *Brix*, a mass ratio of the dissolved sugar. Hand-held refractometers are often carried by grape growers to do quick field measurements.
rootstock	The root system beneath the soil that is tolerant of specific pests or soil conditions. Most grape varieties are *grafted* onto rootstocks; it makes no difference in the root's performance as to which *variety* is grafted to the rootstock.
rosé	A light colored semi-red wine made from any red grape. The wine is *short-vatted* to minimize the wine's contact with the *must* after the fermentation process.

SCGGA	Acronym for Sonoma County Grape Growers Association, representing wine grape growers in Sonoma County. A SCGGA winegrape commission was formed in 2006, replacing the earlier-formed SCGGA. The organization was renamed and is now called the Sonoma County Winegrowers Association.
sensory evaluation	A step-by-step process followed to assess a wine's appearance, aroma, body, taste, and persistence in the mouth. The evaluation pays little attention to psychological or any other bias that may arise during wine tasting.
shatter	The phenomenon wherein a grape cluster fails to develop into maturity, caused by harsh climate conditions, often resulting in a failure to pollinate; if the weather is too cloudy or cold or temperatures are too high, the vine's flowers remain closed, preventing pollination and development of fruit.
shoot	A new green stem that sprouts from a vine in the spring of the growing year, which, if allowed to continue to grow, will likely produce leaves and possibly fruit.
short vatted	Means the grape skins are allowed to ferment with the freshly pressed grape juice (the must) for only a short period of time, as opposed to long-vatted, which means the skins are kept in contact with the skins for a longer time. Short-vatting is how rosé wines are made.
shot berries	The few small, seedless grapes sometimes found in an otherwise normal bunch of wine grapes, caused by improper fertilization during the normal blooming and pollination period.
situs	Refers to location; in the case of a grape vineyard, refers to the specific character of the location, be it geographical or peculiarities of the location.

smudge pots	Portable outdoor heating units fired by an oil, such as diesel or kerosene; formerly used extensively in vineyards to elevate temperatures at ground level to prevent frost that could seriously damage grape vines. Their use has been prohibited for the past several decades owing to their contributions to local air pollution.
SO₂	Sulfur dioxide, a gaseous compound injected into aging wine to maintain control of microorganisms and absorbed oxygen. In some places, it is written SO2.
sparging	A process for removing air (oxygen) from an empty wine bottle by injecting nitrogen into the bottle prior to filling with wine.
St. George rootstock	A wine grape *rootstock* imported from a proprietary Italian source that is resistant to *phylloxera*. This rootstock has been planted extensively in the Forchini vineyards.
Stopper (*bung*)	Usually of wood or plastic, formed to fit into a *bung hole*; used to shut off the contents of a barrel from outside air; usually of a porous nature to allow gas (*CO₂*) buildup from aging of the barrel contents to escape, rather than blow the *stopper* out of the bung hole. The stopper is generally referred to as a *"bung."*
sucker	Suckers often arise from buds at underground node positions on the trunk of a vine. Sucker shoots are usually removed early in the season before the buds on the suckers can mature. Above-ground suckers are typically stripped off the trunk manually so a pruning stub does not remain to harbor additional latent buds that could produce more suckers in the following year. Suckers rob an established vine of the water and nutrients that the established vine needs.
suckering	The removal of *suckers* during the pruning process.
sugar stand	In a winery entryway, a station at which a grape delivery vehicle stops in order for the winery testers to test the sugar content (*Brix*) of the grapes being delivered.

tannin/tannic	Chemical compounds (phenols) that come from the skins of grapes; the tannins have much to do with the astringence of a wine, contributing to whether the wine is great or poor. A tannic wine possesses tannins that have not been tamed, so much that the tannins overpower the taste of the wine.
thief/thieving	Refers to a wine thief, which is a tube-shaped tool that is dipped into a *fermenter* or barrel to extract a portion of developing wine.
toasted barrel/ head	Charring the inside of a new, or relatively new, wood barrel over an open flame to caramelize the surface of the barrel interior and impart to a stored wine some desired flavor of the toasted barrel.
topping the barrel	Replacing wine that has evaporated from within a barrel during aging, so that the stored wine does not become oxidized by contact with air in the void left by the evaporated wine or shrink too much in volume.
trellis	In a vineyard, typically a system of wires strung between posts and/or articulated frameworks, to which vine arms are fastened and on which new vine growth develops. The trellis supports the vine, keeping the vine off the ground, untangled, and better exposed to air and sunlight.
trellis planting	A vine planted with a *trellis* on which the vine is trained to grow. The trellis usually creates a row of vines, and a corridor is left between rows of vines through which machinery and personnel can move. This style of planting is common for most varieties other than stout-trunk old vine Zinfandel, which has been trained by *head-pruning*.
variable capacity tank (VCT)	A small tank for holding a quantity of wine that is used to top off barrels during the barrel-aging process.
varietal	A wine made from a single *variety* of grape. Current regulation requires a minimum 75% of the named variety to use this label.
variety	A type of grape; for instance, Cabernet Sauvignon, Merlot, Chasselas, or Pinot Noir.

West Dry Creek Ranch	The second of three Forchini vineyard properties, located at 9182 West Dry Creek Rd. in the upper reaches of Dry Creek Valley. No residence was established at this location.
willow wrap	Flexible shoots from a willow tree, used by some *winegrowers* to fasten portions of a vine to the posts of a *trellis*; used instead of twine, plastic ties, or other artificial fasteners.
winegrower	A person who owns or works in a vineyard or winery, or one who cultivates grapes to be made into wine.
witching (dowsing)	Dowsing and water witching are defined as the act of locating ground water or underground streams through the use of a divining rod. Water witching is the oldest form of dowsing.

Acknowledgements

THIS SHORT BOOK is a personal memoir of James Franklin (Jim) Forchini. It was written by him as a tribute to his wife, Anita, who predeceased him by nine months, in March 2021. Jim's other purpose was to set forth, in writing, the story of his development as a winegrower, primarily for the benefit of his family and friends. His hope was that his story might inspire their lives as well.

Before Jim died suddenly in January 2022, he had completed drafting his story, covering his life up to the production of the first vintage from his new winery in 1996. Addressing the last 24 years of his story has fallen to the editor of this book. Working under the direction of his surviving children, all now grown adults leading their own lives, the summary of those final years has been written to conclude Jim's story. It is hoped that Jim would approve of what the epilogue includes, and how it has been said. We will never know for sure, but we can imagine that he would.

All the photography contained within these pages was extracted from Jim's vast collection of photographs. He must have been fascinated with cameras, particularly the iPhone camera with which he, no doubt, took most of the photographs in the last 10-15 years.

The few maps in the book were prepared by the editor using the GoogleMap GIS geographic information system software. Images were annotated to help support the story Jim was telling in the text of the chapters in which the maps appear.

The editor's arrangement with Jim's children was to edit the draft material left by Jim, incorporating everything he wrote into a narrative that could be easily read and enjoyed by his readers. Jim had admonished that this was his story, told in his way; he essentially defied anyone to change anything. Yet some editorial revisions have been made to help make the story more accessible to a wider readership. But none of the revisions detract from the content or the spirit of Jim's tale, and Jim's style of storytelling has been preserved.

Carla Forchini, Jim's daughter and the middle of the three siblings, has been the principal contact during preparation of this book. She ensured that all known draft text written by Jim was available, and she furnished Jim's extensive library of photographs. Since Jim never completed assembling this library, most of the photographs were unidentified. The subjects of some photographs have never been determined, but Carla has done what she could to properly identify everything that has been used in the book. Carla also reviewed each chapter, and provided extensive comments on the epilogue, which was drafted by the editor at her request.

The entire book was reviewed by Dr. James O'Brient, a geologist from Moraga, California, with an interest in winegrowing and terroir. Also, as a winemaker on a very small scale, he had a natural interest in the book and how the Forchinis' story unfolded. As a personal friend of the editor, he consented to lend his literary talents to a review of the entire text, proofreading everything within. His contribution is much appreciated,

Publication of the book was done by Linda Roghaar of White River Press, Amherst, Massachusetts. Of particular note is the work of Doug Lufkin, who has handled all design and layout, and has ensured that the quality of each image is adequate for printing. Doug has a long record of producing books of exceptional quality and taste, including several for the editor. Doug and Linda's work here is much appreciated.

Jim Forchini's primary interest was to honor his beloved wife, Anita. His story was dedicated to her for her faithful love and companionship during their 60 years of life together. They followed their dreams and built an enterprise consistent with their vision. This small book helps memorialize their journey.